KINGDOM RACIAL CHANGE

Kingdom Racial Change

Overcoming Inequality, Injustice, and Indifference

Michael A. Evans
David L. McFadden
Michael O. Emerson

William B. Eerdmans Publishing Company
Grand Rapids, Michigan

Wm. B. Eerdmans Publishing Co.
2006 44th Street SE, Grand Rapids, MI 49508
www.eerdmans.com

© 2025 Michael A. Evans, David L. McFadden, and Michael O. Emerson
All rights reserved
Published 2025

Book design by Leah Luyk

Printed in the United States of America

31 30 29 28 27 26 25   1 2 3 4 5 6 7

ISBN 978-0-8028-8372-8

Library of Congress Cataloging-in-Publication Data

A catalog record for this book is available from the Library of Congress.

Contents

Prelude ... 1

Part 1. Telling the Stories amid National and Local Realities

1. We Were Children ... 7
2. Boys to Men and Getting Saved ... 25
3. Getting Down, Getting Out ... 49
4. Grown-Up Times ... 73

Interlude ... 103

Part 2. Making Kingdom Racial Change

5. Make No Small Plans—Macro-Level Change ... 107
6. The Meso-Level Change Levers ... 128
7. Healthy Micro-Level Worlds and God's Love Offensive ... 144

Postlude ... 163

Building Blocks of Kingdom Racial Change ... 169

Bibliography ... 171

Index ... 175

Prelude

On a summer afternoon in 2024, more than 180 Christian men from across the Chicago area gathered at Guaranteed Rate Field (what a name) for the annual crosstown rivalry game of the Chicago Cubs and the Chicago White Sox baseball teams. These men—about half Cubs fans, about half Sox fans—came together not only from across Chicagoland but from several different racial communities, different churches, and lifetimes of different experiences. For this day, they tailgated together, they talked with one another, and they prayed together. Then and only then did they go into the stadium together to witness a baseball game.

They were brought together as part of the Unity movement, founded and run by two men—two of the authors of this book—Dr. David McFadden (Dr. David) and Rev. Michael Evans (Rev. Ev.). Both grew up on the south side of Chicago, in rough neighborhoods. Odds say they should be on the streets, in prison, or dead from violence or a drug overdose. That they would grow up to start and lead a local multiracial movement for racial justice and unity is improbable, a testament to God's power and a model for how we can move from being racial tribes to a Christian family, the very reality God proclaims.

We know there are amazing, God-inspired books by Christian authors addressing how we can overcome racial issues that have plagued our nation and have divided and harmed the church. This book will expand on those books in important and unique ways, combining four components to produce a novel work that can encourage and inspire you.

We are all attracted to story. Jesus taught with stories—parables—that connected the here and now to larger truths and what should be. An important component of this book is relying on telling our stories, those of the three authors, to make larger points about God's creation.

Prelude

Two authors—friends since grade school—grew up in the rough neighborhoods of Chicago's south side. One now serves as a medical doctor, and the other ministered in the very neighborhoods where he was raised. The other author—Michael Emerson, who is white—grew up in a white world, sometimes physically just a few miles from Dr. David and Rev. Ev. and sometimes not, but always socially a world away.

Because Emerson is a professional sociologist, a second component of our book is that as we tell our stories, we step back and look at the sociological contexts, drawing on research to situate our stories and understand larger realities. We draw on data local to our stories and data from the national context. For example, when we talk about where we lived growing up, we situate our stories in data, which helps us understand the neighborhood, city, and national realities of the time. Doing so helps us all contemplate if our stories are unique to us or if they are illustrative of fundamental trends shaping us all. We also draw on sociological theory, which helps us make sense of our stories and the larger contexts to which the data point. We shall consider life at the multiple levels in which it occurs: at the micro level (individuals, relationships, families), the meso level (organizations such as churches and collective activities such as social movements), and the macro level (entire institutions such as the criminal-justice system or the educational system, as well as laws and policies). We experience these levels almost every day of our lives, though we rarely give them direct thought. We must consider these levels, in turn, and how they are interrelated if we are to make progress in kingdom racial change.

What do we mean by *kingdom racial change*? If you have ever thrown out your back or had back problems so severe that you could neither stand straight nor walk, you know that you need a realignment to be right again. Short of such a realignment, you exist in severe pain, unable to function normally or perhaps even at all. Our nation has thrown out its collective back so severely that it is crippled, curled up into a shadow of what it should be. We desperately need a realignment to be right again with God's intentions for his people. Kingdom racial change is the sum total of the processes that must occur for us to get back into biblical, godly alignment across racial groups. It is overcoming racial inequality, injustice, division, and indifference. It is arriving at justice, righteousness, reconciliation, unity, and community.

A core third component is that this book is biblically guided. Stories and sociological analysis are ultimately only insightful if they are

Prelude

informed and guided by biblical teaching. We rely on God's Word as we write this book, and as such, we take clear normative stances. Some things are right, some things are wrong. And this is because God's Word declares it so. We know there are many gray areas in the world, yet on the topics discussed in this book, we have straightforward teaching to guide us down a clear path. We use the NIV translation in this book.

The first half of the book uses these components to identify eleven essential *building blocks* for change. The building blocks lead, then, directly into our final component of the book: outlining the principles for change where we have veered treacherously from God's clear path. If we desire to get back on the path, how can we do so? In the second half of the book, we arrive at biblically rooted, sociologically nested, and experientially tested principles that can have Christians of all different hues working together for God's kingdom. This is what we were designed to do.

Satan warps us, Satan confuses us, and Satan violently rips us off of God's path of justice, reconciliation, and unity. Satan sadly often does this with the very relationships needed to address the issues. God provides not only the call but also the clear means for overcoming Satan's division and injustice. We absolutely must work together. Therein is the power. Why are we so separated after hundreds of years by race and class and related issues? Because if and when we are not, if we become unified in our devotion and service to God, Satan is a goner. Satan knows this better than us. And this fact is why Satan's desire for division among Christians is insatiable and relentless.

What a joy and privilege to be called to work with God to overthrow the darkness. What a joy and privilege to be called to work with God for the endless shining of God's saving and loving light. We have such a grand purpose given to us by our Lord. We shall struggle, we shall feel down at times, and we shall even experience episodic losses. But God has already told us the outcome. God wins! God's people unite. God's people live in a beloved community. So, with energy, with confidence in the outcome, and with our faith, we continue upon this great work, the very work God has called us to with whatever years on earth we have.

In short, this book considers how Christians—those whose highest allegiance is to Christ and whose highest goal is to be Christ-like—can face the reality of racial evil and overcome it. We can and will improve lives, organizations, and institutions so that all are more Christ-like, allowing the flourishing of God's creation. During his time on earth,

Prelude

Jesus talked an incredible amount about the kingdom of heaven. In fact, most of his parables were to illustrate what the kingdom of heaven is like. And he taught us to pray for that kingdom to come to earth just as it is in heaven. That is why this book is called *Kingdom Racial Change*.

We begin our journey by going back in time to the 1960s, when the authors were born. Time travel has its privileges, and time travel we shall do. We invite you now to join us, to see what we learn together.

PART 1

Telling the Stories
amid National and Local Realities

1

We Were Children

Three unique lives, situated within three families, two racial groups, and one nation. All three of us are Christian, all three of us are men, all three of us are roughly the same age, all three of us are married with children, and all three of us live in the United States. Two of us are African American (Evans and McFadden), and one of us is white (Emerson). In this chapter, we focus on essentially just one year of our childhood, the same year. Doing so brings into relief both our similar and our different contexts. The lessons garnered from comparing our lives during this year constitute a vital first step toward moving to kingdom racial change. We shall tell each of our stories in turn and then compare our stories to see what we learn, putting them into the context of larger national trends. By using this approach, we create the *building blocks* we shall put to use in the second half of the book. The essential building block we will arrive at through what we learn in this chapter is this: *The mighty arm of racial power is that it is systemic (Building Block 1)*. What this means and why it matters so greatly will become clear as we move through the chapter.

Rev. Michael Evans (Rev. Ev.)

The year was 1967. It was April, my fifth birthday had just passed, and this was the night I learned that my life would change forever.

We lived in San Francisco, California. My father, David Luke Evans, worked as a machine mechanic during the day and was in seminary at night studying to become a minister like his father and his father before that. He would become the third generation of ministers just as three of his seventeen (yes, seventeen) siblings had already done.

Part 1. Telling the Stories amid National and Local Realities

On that night, my father called us all in the living room for a family meeting. Family meetings meant my mother, Edith, my dad, and me and each of my six siblings must be in the room before the first word would be spoken. Of my siblings, three were older than me, and three were younger. I had to learn how to deal with my older siblings, who could sometimes be hard on me for playing around too much. I had to learn how to work with my younger siblings, who relied on me as their big brother.

Family meetings were always serious. My father was a strict disciplinarian. No talking, no playing, no laughing, and absolutely no giggling was allowed. All of those things were signs of disrespect to the speaker. And since my father was the speaker, you made sure to give him your undivided attention. Silence and paying attention were the only ways to survive a family meeting. Now, when you put nine people in a small room and seven kids with one very serious speaker, something was bound to happen—laughter, a giggle, a poke, a hit, or maybe a note passed around. God help us if we did any one of a hundred things that could cause us to lose control and get us all in big trouble.

It became customary to keep my sister Donnie and me apart from each other. We were trouble just waiting to happen. Now, as an adult, Donnie is the smallest of my siblings, but back then, she towered over me. She used any of our family meetings as a good time to pick on me. She could make me laugh or cry, whatever she chose at the time, which could cause hearing the words we most dreaded spoken by my father: "Line up!" That meant everyone had to get in line by age and get a whipping, never just one of us, but all of us. My father always had a specific number of swats he planned to divvy out on our butts only. It ranged from two to five licks, depending on the severity of the offense. He had an incredible knack of hitting you in the exact same spot with each lick applied. If we all had to get a whipping for whatever reason, sometime later after the family meeting and the whippings were over, my brother and sisters and I would come back together and decide who caused us all to get punished. That person or persons would get the wrath of all the siblings. Donnie and I were always the usual suspects. So we were kept apart at the beginning, just for us to have a chance to make it through a family meeting.

But this meeting in the spring of 1967 was perhaps the most memorable and certainly the most impactful. On this night, we learned we would be moving to Chicago, the place I had always heard about. We were shocked and disoriented. The suddenness of my father's announcement raised many unspoken questions, mainly, *Why?*

But like I said, the questions would have to remain unasked until my father said, "If you have any questions, I will take them now." That would only come after he would say, "Mother, did you have anything you wanted to add?" Neither of those times arrived tonight. My twelve-year-old brother and ten-year-old sister (the two oldest) seemed furious. But my father was not asking us if we wanted to move to Chicago. He was telling us we were moving to Chicago and doing so immediately.

The decision was made. Before he opened the floor for questions or let my mother add any of her thoughts, my father did give us his reason for making this life-changing family decision: it was time to go back home to where my father was from. That was it: it was time. He had already informed his employers he was leaving and had already dropped out of seminary.

After asking my mother if she had anything else to add (she didn't), he opened the floor to us. Most of the questions were actually expressions of anger, and "Why couldn't you wait until the school year was over?" More was said, but I had just turned five and did not understand all that was happening.

Believe it or not, Chicago was the place I saw most days of my young life on TV. Before cable and streaming, channels were local, except for one or two "super stations" broadcast nationally, the main one being WGN from Chicago. Channel 9 was our WGN "super station." From watching it, I felt like I knew as much about Chicago as I knew about my home of San Francisco, maybe more.

You see, our TV was fixed on Channel 9 with no exceptions when my father was home. We could turn the channel when my father was at work or school. But before he walked in the door, Channel 9 had better be on, or the TV was off. The spring and summer months were dominated by Cubs baseball. We had to know enough of what happened in the games to hold a good conversation. My father was a diehard Cubs fan, and they played only daytime home games back in those days. Because of that and the fact that we were two hours behind Chicago time, my father could not actually watch the games during the week. Thus, I was made the official Cubs game watcher, which I considered a true honor. My job was then to provide my father a game summary when he came in the door (think of me as my father's 1960s internet!). As a young kid I learned names like Ernie Banks, Billy Williams, Ron Santo,

Part 1. Telling the Stories amid National and Local Realities

and Fergie Jenkins, as well as all the other players and their positions on the field. They were like my friends. I knew more about the Cubs players than I knew about most of my own relatives. And since I knew none of my relatives outside my family, that was a sad truth. Maybe that had a lot to do with the reason my father decided we should all go back to Chicago.

The day for us to make our way across the country to Chicago arrived too soon. As much as I did not like the idea of leaving my friends behind, I had to admit I began to look forward to seeing in person the place I only knew from TV. Just to be in the place where my parents said in the winter you can make snowmen and have snowball fights made me excited. It seemed to my five-year-old self that the fun we would have in this new snow stuff far outweighed whatever problems might come with the package deal. My father made sure to show us on a huge map how far we had to go from California to Illinois, and all the places in between. It seemed like a daunting task.

Only now would my mother openly express what she needed to say about our journey. She wanted us to first stop in Detroit, even though it was several hundred miles further east, before we settled in Chicago. Detroit is where my mother was from, and it is where she and my father met.

My father said, "Sure thing, honey. First we stop in Michigan, then we make our way to Illinois and Chicago." No one could get my father to change something he had already said except my mother.

We could not take many items on this life-changing journey, only the bare necessities. My father did all the driving. He always stayed north of the Mason-Dixon line while we drove. He never dipped south for any reason. There was too much of a chance for trouble if we went too far south. In many of the southern states, we could not go into rest stops or restaurants in the 1960s. Even if we did stop at some place to eat or rest, my father would first purposely check the license plates of the cars in the lots to make sure there were not too many southern-state plates.

I was young, but these were my first indicators that we were not welcomed at all places as Black people. I felt how uncomfortable my father was when he saw cars from the southern parts of our country. He never wanted us to hear people making racial comments about his Black children or wife. My father was a very calm man but took very little from anyone who might have threatened his family.

We Were Children

After many days, we finally made it to Michigan. Aunt Betty's place is where we would stay; she was my mama's sister who was eight years older than her. Aunt Betty had practically raised my mother when their own mother died from complications soon after my mama was born. Aunt Betty was a no-nonsense lady but also one of the nicest people you ever wanted to meet. She was firm but fair. Her husband, Uncle Benny, was a very kindhearted man who thought the world of my father. He once told me that my father was the smartest Black man he knew.

While visiting Detroit, we were going to stay a few days with Aunt Betty and Uncle Benny, maybe meet a few more of my mother's relatives while there, and then move on to Chicago. But a few days turned into weeks. April became May, and May became June, and still we remained in Detroit.

We met more of my mother's siblings and many more of our cousins. At the end of June, my father told us in one of our famous family meetings that he had found our family an apartment... in Detroit. *Say what? Chicago is still our goal, right?* When July rolled around, we were all moved into a huge building with many other families. I found out what living in an apartment was, and it was quite different from our house in San Francisco. To live with so many other families so close to us frankly cramped my energetic young lifestyle. We were always told to keep quiet and stop walking so loudly. We were on the second floor, and a family lived right under us.

Do you have any idea how to get seven kids to walk or run quietly? Things were so strange now, and Chicago seemed so far away that it was nearly out of my sight and mind. Things took a serious turn for the worse when my mother sat us all down and told us we needed to get enrolled in school. That meant I was going to kindergarten and had to join the older siblings. It was mid-July, and school started in mid-August in Detroit.

Turns out Grandaddy Fulton still had a few connections at the Ford plant and was able to help get my father a new job there. Hence, Detroit was not just a stop-through anymore; it was our family's new home. *What's the baseball team in this city? And can we please find a place to live that is not so close to another family?* I realized as a kid I needed more space to run and have fun and not get in trouble so much for what I always did; running and jumping around was my life. We needed space!

My mother walked us all to my aunt Betty's house to drop off the youngest three and take the oldest four to the nearest school to enroll us as students. I would be in kindergarten. Wow, school—this was so different from being at home. When school started in a few weeks we would have to walk the near mile ourselves to school. I was not looking forward to that. But I would have no choice in the matter. It was coming, and I had to prepare myself.

The time for school to start was coming much too soon. I was still far from adjusted to living in such close proximity to other families. I could not remember getting in so much trouble in my young life. "Michael, you must be quiet." I heard that one hundred times a day. Or at least it felt like I was told that so often. But ball bouncing and throwing is really what got me in the most trouble.

Apartment life was no fun at all. And to make matters worse, it was time to start school, and it was mid-August hot. I was in school with my older siblings, but I couldn't help but cry to be away from my younger sisters. It didn't help that the younger siblings cried too. We were a mess, but I made it off for my first day. It was only half-day kindergarten, so Aunt Betty would pick me up from school on her way home from work. My mother would pick up my younger siblings and me from Aunt Betty's house, and we would all walk over to the apartment together. My older siblings would just come home to the apartment after school was over. For two weeks, we repeated this routine each day. But by the third week, my father called a sudden family meeting.

He brought us together and told us only this: he'd gotten into an incident at his new job and decided this new arrangement was not going to work. He would be leaving that job immediately, and we would now finally be moving to Chicago. No questions would be entertained, and we would not have any further discussion on the subject. He wouldn't even ask my mother if she had any words to add. He simply said, "Have all your things packed by Friday. We leave Saturday morning for Chicago."

Michael Emerson

While Rev. Ev. was traversing the nation to his new temporary home in Detroit, I was two and a half years old and also living in the city of Detroit. Born in Evanston, just outside of Chicago, my father had taken a job at Ford Motor Company (where Rev. Ev.'s father briefly worked at the same time, though they never met), and we moved to Detroit when I was but one month old. Living upstairs in a two-flat in Detroit, the environment was familial amid Italian neighbors and relatives. My maternal grandparents are from Italy, and at this time, most of my relatives and our family friends were immigrants or the first generation to be born in the United States, such as my mother. Though "ethnic," my mother was "assimilating" by marrying a Norwegian American whose family had been in the United States for several generations. In so doing, she had evidence of "making it" in America. My father, recognizing the importance of the Italian social network and culture for my mother, deferred to her wishes for our living situation. This became all the more important as our family welcomed a second son, my brother Rick. My mother was home full-time raising us, while my father provided for us through his white-collar, college-degree job.

We lived in an all-white world, ethnic though it was, an eternity away from Rev. Ev.'s family and race troubles. Or so we thought. Though Detroit was 30 percent African American at the time, we did not encounter any non-white people, except when going downtown. Our neighborhood was white, as were the surrounding neighborhoods. Our Catholic parish was Italian-white. The police were white (citywide, 93 percent were white; locally, all were white). Everyone at our park was white. Everyone in the stores was white. Our doctor was white. Our dentist was white. The same was true for who we saw in restaurants and for who we visited. I was too little to know then that I lived in a white world. I simply lived in the world, and the world was white. People like Rev. Ev. and his family were not on my family's radar, and our chances of ever meeting in Detroit were essentially zero.

In late July, during this tumultuous, "long hot summer of 1967," riots came to Detroit. Caused by an unlicensed, after-hours police raid of a bar in an African American area, what was unfolding in our city would become the worst riot in the United States since the 1863 New York Draft riots. For five long days and nights, racial tensions that I had zero ability at that time to comprehend erupted. Arson, assault, violence, looting, protest, and killing ensued. When it was finally over—it took calling in the 82nd Airborne Division, the 101st Airborne Division, and the Michigan Army National Guard—43 people were dead (including 16 police officers and military officials and 27 civilians), over 1,110 people were injured, more than 7,200 arrests had been made, and over 400 buildings were destroyed. Detroit sat in smoldering ruins in significant chunks of the city.

Part 1. Telling the Stories amid National and Local Realities

My parents watched the television in horror. In their mind, they had brought their young sons to what they now decided was a city far too dangerous, no longer insulated from racial troubles occurring across the nation. People like Martin Luther King Jr. were, to them, the ultimate instigators of such violent turmoil. In the view of my parents and everyone they knew, the local Black folks were thugs, too lazy to be working and thus with too much time on their hands to have too many children and engage in senseless violence, destroying their very own city.

It took my parents perhaps three weeks to make our move, which we did with several relatives and friends, setting up a new location for the ethnic enclave. And we did not move randomly. We moved directly to a Detroit suburb with signs such as "We want white residents in our white community." The mayor of this suburb had gone on record saying he only wanted white people and invited the white residents to arm themselves to keep it that way. My father, a veteran of the US military, was armed and gladly accepted the invitation. In my parents' view, their first job was to provide a safe environment for their young children, and that meant de facto living in an all-white environment. The nation was going insane. At least this suburb—its mayor, its leadership, and its residents—had the wherewithal to keep that insanity out.

Because the Detroit riot was so significant in my family's life and was indeed historically momentous, I was puzzled that Rev. Ev. does not even mention it in his account of that year. We both lived in the same city at the same time, so how could it not even be worth noting? I had to know, so I asked him if his family also moved due to the riot. He did not know, so he contacted his mother. His text message to me is telling of our different worlds: "My mother remembers the '67 riots. But she said that was not the reason we left Detroit. Black Americans were mad because of discrimination in most major cities. Leaving Detroit for another city would not change that or provide a new reality. Rather, we moved because my father decided to pursue a possible job in Chicago." Whereas my family could plan its escape from racial troubles, such was not even possible to consider for Rev. Ev.'s family.

David McFadden (Dr. David)

While Michael Emerson was born in the Chicago area and left for Detroit, and while Michael Evans had left Detroit for Chicago, I had spent my entire life—seven years by 1967—in Chicago. It was all I knew. But I did not really know Chicago as a whole. What I knew was the isolated, large housing project in which I was born and raised, called Altgeld Gardens, on Chicago's far south side.

Altgeld Gardens consists of seventeen blocks of row apartments. Each block has about one hundred row apartments. Each apartment has one to three bedrooms. My two brothers, my mother, and I lived in a two-bedroom apartment with one bathroom, a small kitchen, and a small living room. Hundreds of families were compacted in these small spaces with paper-thin walls, leaving little privacy. We could easily hear neighbors' conversations on either side of the walls. Often, when I was trying to read, I had to deal with the loud music played by the neighbors.

The condition of the apartments and grounds was fair at best. The utilities were often poor. The furnace system was so ineffective at providing heat during the long, cold Chicago winters that we had to resort to using our oven for heat. Rodents were frequent and unwelcome visitors. When leaving our apartment, we learned to quickly shut the door to prevent rats from entering. I remember our patchwork furniture being so dilapidated that I felt ashamed and embarrassed. Over time, we became desensitized to these conditions, and it became the norm because other children in the neighborhood had similar experiences and acquiesced. Deprivation, setting low goals to no goals at all, confinement, and having the life sucked from you are what these conditions produced.

Even at a young age, I wanted desperately to find a way out of Altgeld Gardens. But I remember promising myself that my sacrificial mother could not be left behind. Like relocating a mountain, the impossible had to be made possible. I had to succeed. I had to find a way to catapult myself out of Altgeld Gardens with my mother.

Our financial state was like essentially everyone else's who lived in our community: poor. Summer vacation, if we got one, was usually a half day at an amusement park or train ride to St. Louis. We purchased our clothes and shoes at low-end or "recycled" stores. Poverty prevailed in all aspects of my young life.

My family life became unstable early; my parents separated when I was three. The separation was devastating to me. It was a difficult life economically with my father present, but without him, it seemed impossible. Our future was bleak at best. I could not handle living in that

Part 1. Telling the Stories amid National and Local Realities

environment without a father. I unknowingly began banging my head against the wall when I was asleep. I would nightly wet the bed. I'm sure there were yet other psychosomatic symptoms I portrayed as a result of being fatherless. No child should be fatherless! The consequences can last for generations.

Because of this experience, I began to make promises to myself that I would never grow up to be like my dad. I promised myself I would not have sex before or outside of marriage to avoid promiscuity. This promise I kept, although difficult. I promised myself I would never leave my family. I did not hate my father, but it affected me deeply. My brothers and I often mentioned our father in our bedtime prayers, asking God to bring him back to Christ. We also prayed that our father would move our family out of Altgeld Gardens into a new neighborhood and house so we could live together with our parents—an intact family!

He eventually gave his life back to Christ, but he remarried and purchased a house for his *new wife and family*. I felt like a dog who was given leftovers. I was the scraps. How could a father treat his own blood this way? I had to find a way to forgive him. This is what God would want. Time is said to be a great healer. Time did allow God to mend my angry, broken, tearful, pushed-aside-for-others heart, but more on that later.

My father didn't totally abandon us. He sent some rent money and some money for food so that we did not have to go on public assistance. He would spend time with his sons once a month but not with my mother. We would have to use some of the food money my father gave us to buy clothes and other necessities for my mother. She didn't work in order to stay home with her sons. In hindsight, this was important to her to give us a sense of an intact family to keep us from joining gangs and getting involved with drugs. Oftentimes, when going to grade school, we would have to navigate our way through gang territory. We would sometimes hear gunshots at night between rival gangs. Some of my friends became gang members. Some of them died early in life because of the gangs. The sad thing is, my experience is the "expected" experience of growing up Black. How sad that some children's "normal" life includes having friends and family murdered or sent to prison, and that is perfectly fine to the larger society, as long as it doesn't impact them, as Michael Emerson noted about his own family.

No child should have to live in the environment in which I was raised. I realized, painfully so, that these communities—the projects—were designed to destroy the aspirations of families and, in essence, prevent them from obtaining the American Dream. For most African Americans, it is indeed only a dream and never a reality.

One day, when I was about eight years old, playing basketball in the neighborhood, I noticed that the game suddenly stopped, and everyone ran toward the highway. All the people in the group running were Black because 99.99 percent of the people who lived in Altgeld Gardens were Black. I knew essentially no white people except some of the teachers I encountered in school. Bluntly, my life as a child was Black. I knew nothing else but a Black world. Though I knew it only indirectly, I knew that white folks had a much better life—more money, fancy neighborhoods, more privileges, and easier lives. It was de facto racial apartheid. But I did not yet know of hatred between racial groups.

That changed that day as a youngster playing basketball. As those I was playing basketball with sprinted toward the highway, I also saw people running out of their apartments toward the highway. When I looked toward the highway, there was a white man walking from his broken-down car. What happened next shocked me.

Our neighbors began to beat the man until I could no longer watch. They then rampaged his car prior to the arrival of the police. I later learned that there was an intense hate for white people by the Black people in my neighborhood. I learned whatever the horrible treatment they perpetrated on that white man, Black people received ten times worse if they were found walking through the Caucasian Roseland neighborhood a few miles away. I don't just think this; it happened several times.

Generational atrocities that have occurred to our people, such as murder, rape, unwarranted incarceration, lynching, constant dehumanizing, and being confined for four hundred years, all led the Black members of my community to charge at the white, harmless man in need because they viewed him as partly responsible for the atrocities they had generationally experienced and for the conditions in which we all now lived.

In the views of people in my neighborhood, every white man in this country was involved in the atrocities that occurred to Black people. Because these atrocities toward Black people were still present, I early on came to realize that I was Black and that certain rules, laws, and perceptions applied to me but not to white people. I also realized that I had better learn those rules, laws, and perceptions very quickly to stay alive. I understood why my family and so many other families found themselves in these poor living conditions. The color of our skin was the single most important factor.

Reflection on Our Young Lives

The three of us "crossed paths" growing up in that we lived in the same cities (Detroit for two of us, Chicago for all three of us), but the chances of us all actually crossing paths across race were, in effect, zero. Because two of us are African American and one of us is white, and because of the complex system of segregation by race and class, our families did not and would not live in the same neighborhoods or sections of the city. We were born into a system we had nothing to do with. But that system ensured that, across races, we could not become friends and we would not live similar lives.

We have focused in this chapter largely on a single point in time, 1967–1968. It may seem a long time ago for folks born after those years. For those born before those years, it is but a blink ago. Our stories reflect the realities of the time. Emerson, the white member, lived as most white folks did then and do now—in a middle-class family with a mom and dad and at least one college-educated parent. He lived in protected white ethnic areas of the city and in quaint suburban areas near the city. He ended up going to quality schools with almost no crime. He lived in a world where everyone was white. "Non-white" people existed to him, but only occasionally on television, a fleeting sighting downtown, and in caricature narratives told by white people to white people about the deep shortcomings and criminality of non-white people. He and his family never went to the sections of the city in which Michael Evans and David McFadden were growing up. They were viewed by Emerson's parents and by his community as too dangerous, too poor, too far, and understood as places not worth taking notice of.

Meanwhile, although Michael Evans was able to spend a few early years on the West Coast and play with children of different backgrounds, that was but a temporary reality. His experiences in Detroit and, as we will learn in the next chapter, in Chicago were in "Black worlds," just as David's life in Chicago was.

Consider Detroit, where the two Michaels were living in 1967. It was, in reality, two cities—Black Detroit and White Detroit—highly segregated by race, as it remains today. As an adult, Michael Emerson has spent several decades studying racial segregation, especially why it happens and its consequences. For so many of us, because we are born into a reality that already is, we don't give much thought to why things are as they are. They just are. The fact that in the United States almost every single city in the nation with racial diversity is racially segregated doesn't strike most Americans as constructed, odd, or wrong. It just is.

If pressed as to why we have racial segregation, the most common street explanation is that people prefer to live with people like themselves. Let's consider this explanation. It has an amazing assumption: that people "like themselves" is based on race. Why wouldn't this be people who like to ride bikes, people of the same faith, people with long hair, or people with children? That we are satisfied explaining racial segregation with a value-laden assumption based on an artificial categorization of race is stunning. And yet, Americans do so all the time.

This is because we are born into a nation where "race" is understood to have social meaning; that is, race is understood to be associated with culture and a host of other characteristics. From a young age, we come to see the differences among people we meet, but in the United States, we learn to see the racial differences (and how to categorize people into racial groups). Even more importantly, we learn that the "races" are different, and these racial differences can mean a myriad of things at different times and contexts. But in the end, it means that we are more than satisfied explaining racial segregation with a simple "people prefer to be with people like themselves."

So we are caught in a loop: Why do we have racial segregation? Because we want to associate with people like us. Why does "people like us" mean our racial group? Because there is segregation by race, and thus we develop social networks and ways of life that are different. And why, again, do we have segregation? Because we want to be with people like us.

Even if it is true that we want to be with people like us, the amazing fact here is that we so readily accept that "people like us" are determined by our race. And even more amazing is that we can be so okay with that. As Christians, we ought to be horrified. Our Creator teaches us that "people like us" are but one thing—other Christians. They are our family, as we all share the same Father. God never says that we ought to divide by ethnicity, or by the size of our bank account, or by any other characteris-

Part 1. Telling the Stories amid National and Local Realities

tic. We are to be salt and light in the world, even as the world often hates us. Hence we need one another. God has given us one another as support in our mission. But we readily and repeatedly divide our support into factions, accepting racial, economic, and lifestyle segregation as just the way it is. Jesus never accepted "just the way it is." He was a revolutionary, as we are to be—not to overthrow governments or seize power, but to spread the gospel to all and to overturn the world's system of division and hierarchy that places differential value upon people.

But Christians, it turns out, are just as racially segregated from one another as are others. Far from being revolutionary, we simply conform to the ungodly, harmful status quo. Racial segregation arose because of an extensive set of discriminatory laws, policies, and covenantal agreements as to who could live where, who could get loans, and to whom you could sell your home. These laws and policies codified white people's prejudice and made that prejudice the law of the land. Once they were codified, it didn't matter what people personally felt or believed. Over time, however, through sacrificial efforts to change the codification, most of those discriminatory policies have been outlawed with other policies such as the Fair Housing Act and many other laws and rulings.

So, how is it that we still remain racially segregated today? Turns out, most of us simply don't give much conscious thought to race as we engage in our housing search. We know certain areas are not "good" areas, and we avoid them, but we rarely think about why they are not "good" areas, save that they may be seen as high-crime places or places without good schools (but then, of course, we could ask how we know what a good school is). We are looking to live in the "good" areas, which friends, family, and realtors recommended to us. What we don't think about is the system set in place that generates the automatic inertia for racial segregation. What areas do we, our friends, our family, and our realtor know? The ones they live in or have acquaintances in. Because of racial segregation, that means they will know of the areas filled with people of the same race. They will vaguely know of other areas, but because those other areas are so little known, they will not be seriously considered, and no homes in such areas will be toured.

Sociologist Maria Krysan and her co-researcher Kyle Crowder wrote a most impressive book about this process.[1] They argue and show that

---

1. See Maria Krysan and Kyle Crowder, *Cycle of Segregation: Social Processes and Residential Stratification* (New York: Russell Sage Foundation, 2017).

even if we had absolutely no racial prejudice and no discriminatory laws, and even if people were entirely willing to live in racially integrated neighborhoods, it won't happen on any large scale. Our system of racial segregation has been in place too long, and the inertia is simply too powerful to overcome racial segregation. In order to overcome racial segregation, that inertia would have to be disrupted. That might mean people actually, consciously think about race when searching and make it their number-one priority to live in an integrated neighborhood or a neighborhood where they are the racial minority. We all know that is simply not going to happen. Hoping for a massive change of heart and a massive change in housing search priorities, then, is not the answer (in the second half of the book, we will consider what is).

But wait, what is the big deal if we are racially segregated? Does it really matter? As we study the consequences of racial segregation, it quickly becomes clear that segregation matters immensely. Michael Emerson published a summary piece about this called "Residential Segregation Rewards Whites While Punishing People of Color."[2] As noted in that piece, racial segregation is the lynchpin of racial inequality in our nation. It leads to unequal access to education, drives ever wider the huge wealth gap between racial groups, and causes gross inequalities in public services, housing quality, health, life chances, marriage and divorce rates, crime rates, incarceration rates, and so much more. In short, some people (mostly white) gain immensely from racial segregation—more isolation from poverty, keeping crime at bay, nicer parks, and better-funded schools, to name a few—and other people (mostly Black and Brown people) lose substantially from racial segregation. They pay a severe penalty. Think back to David's description of his life earlier in the chapter. His family is an example of paying the penalty.

Recall that he lived in a large housing project called Altgeld Gardens and that it was essentially all African American. Altgeld Gardens was not nearly 100 percent African American by chance. And it was not filled with thousands of poor people by chance. It was literally the requirement for living there. You had to be Black and poor (one of the very few white persons who lived there David knew was interracially married). We have a classic case of racial segregation causing concentrated

---

2. Michael Emerson, "Residential Segregation Rewards Whites While Punishing People of Color," Kinder Institute for Urban Research, Rice University, September 21, 2020, https://tinyurl.com/3arctv5h.

poverty. Concentrated poverty is statistically associated with a host of social ills, such as poor schools, chronic diseases, child sickness, high pollution, gang activity, broken families, poor social services, infrastructural decline, drug addiction, pregnancy out of wedlock, and low life expectancies.

Altgeld Gardens was and is a public housing project run by the Chicago Housing Authority (CHA).[3] Built right at the end of World War II, its nearly 1,500 units cover about 190 acres in the far south of Chicago. It was built by the Department of Housing and Urban Development to provide low-income housing for returning African American veterans, a seemingly honorable purpose, to be sure. But because of the low-income requirement, it created by design (if not intent) concentrated poverty. According to a 1947 CHA report, to be an Altgeld Gardens resident, the family must be African American in a low-income group with a defined maximum income limit (notice here the disincentive—earn too much, and you can't get in or you will need to leave), you must have at least one child under seventeen, your former dwelling must have been substandard, and preference was given to those with the very lowest incomes. What is more, over time the rules came to favor single parents—disincentivizing marriage—and beginning in 1969, a policy was set in place that residents would not pay more than 30 percent of their income for rent. The problem, of course, is this again disincentivized increasing income. In fact, it incentivized unemployment. Make nothing, pay nothing. This led to a difficult feedback loop—less and less rent money meant less and less money available for maintenance, which meant more and more decline.

However, due to how race operates in the United States, the Altgeld housing development was located by design in Black Chicago and was placed on highly toxic land. In fact, Altgeld Gardens is nicknamed the "toxic donut" because it has the highest concentration of hazardous waste sites in the United States. On the land upon which it was built and on the land surrounding, it has 50 landfills and 382 industrial sites, many of which were for decades unregulated, free to dump hazardous waste into the ground and water and free to spew toxins into the air.

---

3. Materials and details about Altgeld Gardens come from multiple sources, including a dissertation by Beverly Anne Lesueur, *Altgeld Gardens: Evolution of Culture and Education in an Isolated African American Community* (diss., Loyola University Chicago, 2010), https://tinyurl.com/2nwssbp9. See also the Wikipedia entry on the housing project, https://tinyurl.com/3c9x58rx.

Over 250 leaking underground storage tanks with toxins have been found. Asbestos was for many years produced in the area.

The result? The highest cancer rates in Chicago. High rates of asthma and respiratory illnesses. High rates of lung and breast cancer. A majority of pregnancies have birth abnormalities. Decaying teeth, high rates of generalized sickness, high rates of missed days of work and school, and extremely low life expectancies. At age ten, David remembers being evacuated from Altgeld Gardens due to toxic fumes encircling the projects. For the entire twenty-three years he lived there, he and everyone else had to deal with a foul smell hanging hauntingly throughout the projects—inside, outside, everywhere—sometimes tolerable, sometimes overpowering.

Amid this backdrop, people are supposed to either pull themselves up by their bootstraps or accept that they are not as worthy as the white folks on the other side of the city living an entirely different reality. As we have seen, David faced the short end of racial segregation daily. He did not create it, but he had to live it because his skin was Black. Interestingly, if he somehow "made it" economically, it meant leaving his neighborhood. If Emerson made it economically, it meant continuing to live in the places where he grew up. So, even with such a seemingly similar outcome, the long arm of racial segregation produces disparate experiences.

The building block for kingdom racial change we learn in this chapter is this: While we may think of race as a question of whether I am personally prejudiced or whether I have some friends of other racial groups, the mighty arm of racial power is that it is systemic (Building Block 1). That it is systemic is the secret to its vast reach, its influence, and its staying power. Racial injustice has been, over decades and centuries, built into our institutions, our systems, our laws, our neighborhoods, our churches, and our social networks. When Jesus calls his followers to take worldly systems and turn them on their heads, he would undoubtedly include the system of racial injustice, as it is daily gouging his people. Christians do not accept ungodly systems—including segregation—as simply the way things are. They change them.

Conclusion

In the late 1960s, we were all young boys, playing, living with family, and learning to grow up. Because of something we had no control over—our

Part 1. Telling the Stories amid National and Local Realities

race—we had different lives, lives shaped by centuries of racial ideology, laws, beliefs, practices, prejudices, and conflicts. Like a card game, we were dealt different hands; but unlike a card game, this was not a game of chance or skill. It was carefully engineered to ensure a better hand for Michael Emerson than for Michael Evans and David McFadden. In cards, we call that cheating.

2

Boys to Men and Getting Saved

None of us remain children. We transition into teenagers. The teenage years, at least in most contemporary societies, are a tumultuous time for so many of us as we seek identity and purpose, try to understand and navigate the world, and move, often not on a straight path, toward full adulthood. During this time, we often have to decide whether to follow God or go our own way. Our experiences and decisions during these years can and do have reverberating effects on the rest of our lives.

In this chapter, we traverse the rest of our growing-up years. As we compare our lives during this season, we again draw out vital lessons both for how race seemingly operates in our nation and about what additional building blocks we will need to move to kingdom racial change. The building blocks our stories illustrate are that every single one of us occupies *a social location* (Building Block 2), the importance of understanding that there are *advantages* for African Americans, not just disadvantages (Building Block 3), and the urgent and essential need to root out the *Religion of Whiteness* from religious communities (Building Block 4). What these building blocks mean and why they matter will be addressed in this chapter through our stories and through our sociological analysis of our stories.

Rev. Ev.

In the last chapter, my story ended with my father informing our family on a Friday that the very next day we would be moving from Detroit to Chicago. Saturday morning arrived and, true to his word, away we went, traveling across Michigan, curving around Lake Michigan in Indiana, and moving on into Chicago. We landed in the Englewood

Part 1. Telling the Stories amid National and Local Realities

neighborhood of south Chicago, still today considered one of the city's most dangerous neighborhoods. Over the next five years, my family and I bounced around from one rental unit to another, always in Englewood. Rampant crime and terrible living conditions were a daily reminder of why it was nearly impossible to make it to adulthood unscathed in Chicago's predominantly Black communities.

Though the neighborhood was deeply poor, dangerous, and had growing drug-use issues, my father was determined to keep my mother and his seven children safe from these negative obstacles and to keep his two sons out of the gangs. The first days living in Englewood community, we saw the potential trouble with gangs in the area. The two largest gangs were the Gangster Disciples and the Black Stones Rangers. The main trouble was in the fight for territory; the gangs were always recruiting new blood into their membership to increase their influence and territory. The bigger your numbers, the better your chances to win an all-out gang war.

My brother Carlos had just turned thirteen years old, but he was tall for his age. The Gangster Disciples had control of the block we lived on. They could not allow the Black Stones to recruit Carlos. The Disciples got very bold and aggressive. When my father went to work, they would send two or three gang members to the front door and demand Carlos be sent out.

My mother would not give in to their demands. She would call the police each time it occurred. Twenty-plus minutes after the fact, the police would come, always loaded with questions but never with solutions. Each time this happened, my mom would tell my father about it when he'd come home from work. He heard the panic and fear in her voice and saw what his children were going through. The young community terrorists had gone too far.

A few days later, my father decided to stay home from work. He got up early, drove the car a few blocks around the corner, and walked back home. He came inside, got a chair, and sat at the front door. He told us all not to go outside until he gave permission.

At about 10:30 a.m., loud pounding began at the front door. Three gang members were shouting demands for Carlos to be sent out. Without words, my father grabbed the bat he kept at the door, burst outside, and with his bat began to beat those three young men! They screamed in pain, and his children started crying inside as they witnessed the beatings. He was fast and brutal, not for a second letting them get a moment to take a breath or speak! After he had thrown the last of the three young men off the front porch, he pointed his bat and said forcefully, "Never again! The next time I will not go so easy on you!"

The three gang members quickly limped away, whimpering and supporting themselves as they went down the street. David Evans, my father, became known as "the Crazy Man who lived in the green house on the corner." Neither Carlos nor I were ever recruited by gangs again. The funny thing is, as much as the gangs went out of their collective ways to avoid our house after that, when they saw my mother coming home from the store with groceries in hand, gang members would often help her to the front porch.

To counter all the negative influences in the community, during the summer months, my parents kept their children in church and various other activities as much as possible. Evangelical Christian Church was the church my family joined. It was a highly unusual church for at least two reasons: (1) in this Black neighborhood, the pastor was white, and (2) the church was racially mixed—70 percent Black, 30 percent white. That is rare today, and back in the 1960s and 1970s, such a racial mix was almost unheard of.

The church also had a Christian school. My three oldest siblings—Carlos, Patricia, and Donnie—were enrolled for the fall. The church and school were essential to help the Evans family make it in the difficult environment of Englewood. The Christian school had no kindergarten, so I had to be enrolled in public elementary schools alone. Because my family moved around many times in the first year of coming back to Chicago, I was enrolled in four different public schools as a kindergartener—one in Detroit and three in Chicago. Not ideal.

When I was ten years old, in 1972, my family moved out of Englewood to a neighborhood further south in Chicago. My parents, after years of searching and struggling, had both found decent-paying jobs, my father at Prince Spaghetti and my mother at Johnson & Johnson factories. The new neighborhood was in the middle of a process known as "white flight." As Black families like mine began moving into white neighborhoods, white families moved out rapidly. Such moves would occur in a matter of months, weeks, and in extreme cases, days. I recall wondering what was so offensive about my family that white people had to run away from us.

Despite the white folks being repelled by my family, our move to a home in a less dangerous neighborhood put my family on a positive trajectory. All the moving around was seemingly, finally behind us.

Part 1. Telling the Stories amid National and Local Realities

But a difficult chapter of Evangelical Christian Church would occur in 1974. The church and the church school were in major trouble. Our white pastor was caught in several adulterous relationships with Black female members. The church elders and congregation wanted him to step down as pastor of the church and as principal of the school. The pastor's family was devastated. He and his wife divorced, and his wife and four children moved back to Florida where they originally were from.

The turmoil was overwhelming. Many of the female members involved changed their names and moved out of state to leave the rampant speculation and whisperings taking place. After months of emergency church board meetings and arguments over legality, the pastor was dismissed.

Many members left the church and school. It wasn't a random exodus. While about 40 percent of the Black members left, all of the white members left. The unique congregation of 70 percent Black and 30 percent white members was destroyed. Paul Evans, my uncle, took over the newly formed church as pastor and also became the new principal of the school.

About that same time, my father began doing evangelistic work throughout the Midwest. We, too, left the church in 1975. Through a relationship with a pastor of a different congregation, Pastor Claud D. Lewis, my family and I soon moved our membership to the Bethel House of Prayer.

There were at least three major differences between Bethel House of Prayer Church and our previous church: (1) it was all Black, (2) it met in the basement of the pastor's home with Sunday school at the park district, and (3) it had a distinct emphasis on the growth of youth membership.

God can and does make good out of bad. Such was the case with our church upheaval. In having to switch churches, I met my best and lifelong friend and partner in ministry, David McFadden, who attended Bethel House of Prayer. Both of us were part of the many activities offered by Bethel: Youth Time Bible study that later became Teen Time, choir, Bible Quizzing, Second Saturday Youth Rallies, overnight campouts, trips to theme parks, Gospel Skating, and many other events specifically centered around youth. Our involvement in these activities drew us closer together and also created many friendships with the other youth of the church.

Boys to Men and Getting Saved

By 1976, it was announced that Bethel House of Prayer would be moving from the basement of Pastor Lewis's house to a closed store on 111th Street in the Beverly neighborhood of Chicago. At that time, the Beverly community was a white neighborhood. This was the single largest step Bethel would take since the church had been started in Pastor Lewis's basement many years prior.

However, having a Black church occupying a recently renovated store in a white neighborhood did not go over well with the local residents. Can I pause for a moment to ask a question? Is it really that horrible if Christians who have dark skin want to worship in a building in a neighborhood where white people live? What is the concern? Clearly, the white community did not see us as Christians first. We were Black, and that meant trouble in their minds, no matter who we actually were as Christ's followers. What a strange, twisted world.

After a few months at that location, the white folks had had enough. The community group of Beverly got together with the City of Chicago and had the area redistricted and zoned for business use only. Our church congregation was ousted. The City of Chicago bought the land the church sat on and had the building torn down. That area became a wildflower garden for fifteen years before a new police department was built on it.

The only good that came from the sudden upheaval was that Bethel now had a bit of financial resources to buy a property we needed and wanted for the church to move forward. With a growing youth program and memberships expanding, Bethel needed to hurry and find a new place to call home. We did hear the message sent clearly to us when we had violated it—we had to limit our search to Black neighborhoods.

At this time, my uncle Paul Evans was experiencing a dwindling church congregation, still not able to recover from the upheaval of the infidelity of the previous pastor. However, the Christian school was experiencing growth in attendance. A school building on 91st and Vincennes Avenue was up for sale. Pastor Lewis and my uncle saw how they could be a great help to each other. Bethel needed a church, and Evangelical Christian School needed a school building. They, in time, were able to work out an arrangement where Bethel would buy the former Evangelical Christian church building on 10 West 110th Street in Roseland while Evangelical (now called Anointed Heirs), in turn, could purchase the property at 91st and Vincennes Avenue. Each of their organizations would be able to get what they needed most.

Part 1. Telling the Stories amid National and Local Realities

These negotiations would be worked out by the end of 1977–1978. Until things got settled, Bethel and Anointed Heirs would share the church building, with Bethel having their Sunday school and church services after Anointed Heirs had theirs. They would work this arrangement until Anointed Heirs and Evangelical Christian School could move to their new location.

During this time, my friendship with David took another huge step. Our involvement at Bethel increased as we deepened our personal relationship with Christ and each other. Both of us became part of the church's leadership. We were placed over ministries at the church. I led the church outreach with David's help, and David led the Teen Time Bible study with my help. We also both served as junior ushers and were two of the first of the youth in the church to preach on a Sunday, me at age sixteen and David at eighteen.

In 1978, my father started his own church, St. Mark Full Gospel Church, serving as pastor. I, of course, joined my family in attending St. Mark. Yet I didn't want to leave Bethel. So I didn't.

Instead, I was part of two churches. St. Mark held its Sunday service and Sunday school from 9:30 a.m. to 12:30 p.m. I was there. I then would hustle over to Bethel House of Prayer for their Sunday school and worship from 1:00 to 3:30 p.m. I was churched, y'all.

I also found time to pursue my other passion: baseball. I made the varsity team as a tenth grader at Bowen High School in 1977. After impressing folks in the preseason, I was named co-captain of the team. At that time, Bowen High was about 60 percent Black and 40 percent Hispanic. Fights broke out almost every day; I do not exaggerate. The police would park two paddy wagons outside the doors of the school daily.

The baseball team was the only sport that had about 50 percent of each race on the team. Every other team was heavily one race or the other. Each year the baseball team would play Washington High School at their field on Chicago's far southeast side. At that time, this area of Chicago was still 85 percent white. It was an overtly racist place. For example, it had signs on trees that stated "Niggers go home!"

Whenever we had to play there, the Hispanic players on Bowen's team would tell the Black players to stay close to them at all times for safe passage. Having white people and white players alike openly hating you and umpires making bad calls on purpose was an overtly clear view of the hate of racism. It was difficult for me to see racism so brazen and deliberate. I had experienced group racism—such as shutting down our church because of who attended it—but now I also experienced people directly hating me, even though they knew nothing about me.

I was a good player, and by my junior year, I was the captain outright. I was also a Christian who loved to share his faith. The team's nickname for me? Preacher. They named me well, as it was my life's calling to be sure, even though, at the time, I thought I also wanted to be a professional baseball player. God had better plans.

Dr. David

My mother was four foot seven. She seemed to me highly vulnerable because she was short and because my father had left us. As a result, I wanted to be a good child and cause no trouble to support my mother. She had her hands full with three young boys in one of the roughest neighborhoods in Chicago.

Still, there were times when I had to fight to survive. When I was ten years old, the children would roll old spare tires we had found through the neighborhood (big fun in our poor neighborhood). I had a tire and enjoyed rolling my tire through the neighborhood.

One day, while wheeling my tire with speed and exhilaration, I was stopped by a much older girl. She took my tire and started wheeling it herself. She flat-out stole my tire, which I so adored. I recall wanting to go home and tell my father, but of course, I could not. And no way was I going to bring this to my mother.

So I left the scene humiliated, embarrassed that a girl, although older, stole what was to me the most precious item I possessed. After returning home and mulling over my stolen tire, I made the decision to stand up to this person. I wasn't concerned with getting the tire back at this point, only standing up to this older tomboy. Determined, I went and found the girl who stole my tire. I stared her in the face while she held my tire. Then I acted. I hit her in the stomach with the hardest punch I could muster. I then ran home at lightning speed, hoping that she would not catch me. After reaching home, sweating with exhaustion, I kept this story to myself. I had to stand up and protect myself, and I did.

In the ghetto where I lived, we had but one grocery store for thousands of residents. The grocery store was small and offered poor produce. To get to a "real" grocery store, we had to engage in a thirty-minute

Part 1. Telling the Stories amid National and Local Realities

bus ride to a white neighborhood to an A&P store there. My mother had serious knee trouble, making it difficult for her to travel to get groceries and carry them back on the bus. So, when we would get food money from my father, my brother and I would take the bus to the A&P, do the shopping, carry the groceries to the bus stop, wait for the bus, take the thirty-minute bus ride back to our projects, and then carry the groceries from the bus stop to our apartment. It was a half-day trip, at the very least.

So, as preteens and teenagers, my brother and I braved the elements to grocery shop for the family. That meant waiting at bus stops in frigid winter temperatures for much of the year, often with blowing snow. At other times it meant standing in the heat and rain. The buses were usually packed and uncomfortable. Sometimes it would take two hours or more for a bus to arrive. And if it were too packed, we would have to wait another one or two hours for the next bus. Many a time we had to stand holding our groceries the entire trip, as no seats were available.

We did this, though, in an attempt to get quality produce that was unavailable to us where we lived. The message was clear—those of us in the projects were not worth even a decent grocery store and a modicum of healthy food. As you might imagine, the main problem in our trips back from the grocery store was not just the weather, crowding, and wait times. It was the constant threat (and sometimes reality) of being robbed or accosted by gang members, such as one notorious person named Crazy Gene, who seemed to thrive on taking others' groceries and taunting them in the process.

One day after leaving the grocery store with needed food for our family, I spotted Crazy Gene running at me. I took off running in extreme fear. My heart was pounding, but my speed shifted to another gear to escape him. I avoided Crazy Gene that day and was able to get the food home to our family. Such was our life.

As I was growing up, I searched hard for a way out of my neighborhood. I wanted to find a way to get my mother and family out more than anything. But by a young age, I was convinced that I was academically inferior to white students in other schools. My parents had not graduated high school. Our school's books were outdated. Our school facilities were poor. So many kids were facing so many difficult situations in their lives that learning was not central. Behavioral problems abounded, and teachers were therefore limited in how much they could teach.

Thus, sports or crime seemed the only viable option for many who lived in my community to succeed financially and get out. In fact, the

Wikipedia entry for my high school lists six notable alumni. All were professional athletes, five in the NBA and one in the NFL. I, too, was driven by sports, chess, and basketball in particular as the vehicle that would transport my mother and me out of Altgeld Gardens. Jesus would eventually show me an alternative route to succeed in life, but for many of my growing-up years, I viewed basketball as the path. I was a good player. Most young players want to be known for how well they score the ball. But I wanted to be known for my defense. I never wanted anyone to score on me, ever. I usually guarded the other team's best scorer. I became known in the city for my defense. In fact, the Chicago papers nicknamed me "Mr. Defense." Though a fine player, and though I received a walk-on tryout with DePaul University, I did not receive a college scholarship. I was not as good a player as my classmate, Terry Cummings, who went on to the NBA, winning Rookie of the Year and scoring nearly twenty thousand points in his professional career. Terry and I had an important bond, which I will return to shortly.

My mother was a Christian, so we became involved with church at an early age. I would say I was born in the church. My mother felt a strong call in her life to minister to the young people in our neighborhood. She would have Bible study with the children of our projects in our apartment every week. Although we were poor, my mother gave of the little we had to the children of the neighborhood. She provided meals along with singing accompanied by her playing the piano. This was one of the first experiences I had with evangelism and sacrificial ministry. The charity my mother displayed during those times would later guide me to give of myself and my finances to others.

I gave my life to Christ when I was nine years old. I remember saying to God, "If you are real, I will give you my life." From that point on, my confidence began to soar because of the newfound faith I had in Christ. God gave me boldness. I started talking to young men in the neighborhood about Christ and inviting them to our church youth program. In high school, on my basketball team, I was instrumental in leading Terry Cummings, the future NBA player, to Christ. He is now a Pentecostal minister, sharing Christ with many people.

As Michael Evans noted earlier, my church—which I still attend—started in the basement of our pastor's home. Eventually, we ended up in the Roseland community of Chicago's south side, where we remain today. At that time, the majority of our church was filled with young people.

Part 1. Telling the Stories amid National and Local Realities

Our pastor, his wife, and his sister designed the ministry for young people. They even had a bus come through our projects to take us to the church. For these reasons, I was very active and radical for Christ at an early age. For example, we would have Bible drills constantly where we would memorize entire chapters as children and compete with other churches in quoting the Scriptures. Missionary Blanch Lewis mainly taught this. She spent half of her time in Liberia, Africa, and the other half at her home church on the south side of Chicago.

Our pastor trained us to present the gospel when we were children. I would spread the gospel in grade school and high school. My best friend at that time, Anthony Harris, and I would approach people while they were playing dice, drinking alcohol, or playing basketball. We also presented the gospel to gang members. Some of the young people in Altgeld Gardens to whom we witnessed would break down in tears and receive Christ. We called ourselves "gangsters for Christ." We were radical in our witnessing. My friend and I were not transplanted to the ghetto from the suburbs to present Christ; we were indigenous. We were born in the ghetto and, therefore, gained respect from the people in our neighborhood.

During my teenage years, I met another young man who started attending our church. He became and is my best friend, and he has been deeply influential in many of my major life decisions. Those decisions helped guide me academically and in my Christian life. His friendship also helped me choose my wife I have been married to for well over thirty years. Michael Evans is this friend, my closest friend! I have discovered through our friendship that two are better than one. One can put a thousand to flight, but Michael and I can put ten thousand to flight. At Bethel House of Prayer, our pastor, Brother Lewis, would often have Michael, my brother James, and me lead Sunday morning service. We would open the service with prayer, read the opening Scripture, lead testimony service, and even, at times, reluctantly give the morning message.

As an older teen, I helped start the first prayer group at my high school. We would pray in the library. Various inner-city teenagers came together to pray. It reminded me of the story of Pentecost. It was that powerful. We often left knowing that our needs would be met, and hope, which we were not accustomed to, began to flourish like rivers of living water.

My pastor also started the Chicagoland Youth Fellowship, where multiple inner-city churches would gather monthly for various youth activities during the school year. Such activities would include haystack rides, camping, tobogganing, and concerts. Each month during our gathering, a teen would be selected as teen of the month for their exemplary service to Christ. That teen would be given a trophy. I received this trophy twice during my teen years. This would later become the model I would replicate for our now-multiracial men's group. More about that later.

Michael and I were active. We, along with my brother and others, led the youth ministry, taught Sunday school, sang in the choir, ushered, and did janitorial work. My brother and I were also deacons at our church. Looking back, my growing-up years were the most powerful years of my Christian life. Those early years shaped, navigated, and carried me through the life-shaking trials that I would encounter during adulthood.

My Christian life and the Christian adults around me gave me a new vision and hope—that I could become a medical doctor. Basketball need not be my only hope. I could actually succeed academically, so much so that I could become a medical doctor and help treat people in their physical suffering that I saw all around me. I noted earlier that I had bought the lie that I was inferior, that as a Black child, I simply was not as smart as white children. But God, through his people, helped me fight that lie, a lie that continually attempts to grip me. God helped me make up ground academically by urging me to continually feed myself the Word to keep me in a positive mindset and not give into hopelessness. God, through his people, showed me my ticket was not basketball. It was a vision of becoming a doctor and the academic path that vision required.

Michael Emerson

While Michael Evans and David McFadden were battling life in the neighborhoods left behind by white flight and in the projects, my family's trajectory was influenced by the very same white-flight process, but of course in a highly different way. After our move out of Detroit to an all-white suburb, we lived a life of middle-class, white suburbanites. We did not worry about crime, we were allowed to play throughout the neighborhood, we regularly went to family camps and parks with my parents, and we took vacations to several places.

Part 1. Telling the Stories amid National and Local Realities

In 1970, my father left Ford Motor Company to work for Control Data, at that time a leading company in the rapidly expanding world of computing. The new job meant we moved to Minneapolis, where his company was located. For a few months, we lived in Minneapolis, but soon we moved to a nearby suburb. We moved two more times before I was in fifth grade, each time to a bigger house and nicer suburb. In each case, we lived in communities that were 100 percent white. That was our world, as it had always been, though continually there was the looming "threat" that "diversity" was closing in.

My mother stayed home, raising my brother and me. We loved to play sports and spent lots of time playing outside with neighborhood kids. We built forts (no girls or adults allowed), put playing cards in our bike spokes with clothespins to make it sound like the bike had a motor, and never even heard of gangs. I apparently liked to color, as I won the boy's state championship in coloring for multiple years while in grade school (hard to believe there used to be such competitions). My brother and I also set a record in our area for the most consecutive hours of nonstop seesawing (we called it teeter-tottering). We knew we hit the big time when a reporter arrived, took our picture, and wrote a story in the local paper about our record.

I don't know how much money my father made, but money never seemed to be an issue. We could afford a nice house with a big yard, two cars, vacations, a boat, eating out, buying clothes, and giving gifts. Everyone I knew seemed to be in exactly the same situation. I did not know there were poor people, single-parent families, or rundown neighborhoods. The neighborhoods my family and I lived in were immaculate; people had money, and almost everyone had a mom and a dad.

My brother and I would spend portions of our summer staying with our Italian grandparents (my Norwegian grandfather had died before we were born). Though my father was not Catholic, out of a commitment to a document he signed when he married my Catholic mother, we were raised Catholic, though we did not attend Mass often while living in Minnesota.

In 1975, when Michael Evans's family was going through much church turmoil, my father announced to my mother that he wanted the family to move to a small town away from suburban life so his boys could play multiple sports in high school and, truth be told, so there would be no risk of "diversity" coming our way. Thus, my father and mother jumped at the opportunity when they found a roller rink for sale three miles outside of a small town about sixty miles from the Twin Cities metro area. Still, it was a curious choice given how ethnic my mother was (Italians didn't live in small towns in this part of the country), given that she had never really lived in a small town, and given that there was no Catholic church in the town or surrounding towns. The pull of racial homogeneity (the simple, clean life) was that strong.

Before we knew it, we were living in a house on a lake in a rural area across a dirt road from where the roller rink was located. My father ran the behind-the-scenes operations of the business, while my mother ran the actual sessions, serving as the floor monitor, DJ, and "enforcer" if people misbehaved. The town was nearly all people of Nordic descent (Swedes, Danes, Finns, and Norwegians), with a few people of German descent. These reserved people were scared of my mother (I was told so many times) because she was loud, direct, intense, and talked with her hands.

My brother and I were the "help." We worked at the concession stand, handed out and put away skates, and learned to be very good skaters. I even competed in couples skating competitions (with matching outfits) and appeared on television because we won several times. It was also a great way to meet girls, who were becoming much more interesting to me as I hit puberty. One girl I first met in fifth grade while roller skating ended up being my bride, though I didn't know it at the time. Joni and I have been married since 1986 when we were both twenty-one.

My brother and I did indeed play sports, lots of sports: hockey, football, baseball, tennis, track, and basketball. We also entertained our new sister, who was born when we moved to this small town. She was about eleven years younger than me. After a few years of this life, my father decided to go back to work in computers (the roller rink was not earning the income he had hoped), while he had my mother run the roller rink. For the rest of my growing-up days, he commuted 120 miles a day, every weekday, to his place of employment in Minneapolis and back, often through blizzards during the long winters.

Still he found the time to attend all of our games and to offer counsel about life when we had questions. He painted a vision for me early on that a "best life" would be as a professor at a college in a small town, "where you can walk slow and think big thoughts." That appealed to me. I liked to learn, and the thought of getting paid to do so seemed like quite a deal. Unlike David, I had no inferiority complex planted

Part 1. Telling the Stories amid National and Local Realities

in me that I was not good enough to learn or that I wasn't expected to learn. Quite the opposite. I was expected to achieve academically even though I was a "jock" (the name for guys in sports). My schools had excellent facilities, and I had fine teachers, many of whom encouraged and helped me along the way. I ended up in the National Honor Society beginning in the tenth grade, and that afforded me many opportunities to hang out with smart kids and go on educational trips. I did well on standardized tests, which only made me more interested in learning. I read endlessly. I especially devoured biographies, being fascinated not only by people's lives, but by the fact that they always ended the same—in death (looking back, it was rather morbid, though it taught me the temporariness of life).

Our town had its racial prejudices, which were accepted and part of normal life. We told ethnic and racial jokes. We knew—didn't just think—that blacks, Mexicans, and Indians (the terms we used on a kind day) were inferior. They were inferior because they spoke English incorrectly, had too many babies, weren't as smart as white folks, were drunkards, were lazy, were bent on committing crimes, and the fathers were absent. They were uncontrolled and, therefore, uncivilized. They were the standard of what not to be.

For example, my brother was for our area a very good basketball player. He played point guard and could dribble in fancy ways, with many moves that allowed him to drive in for acrobatic shots, which he usually made. In one particular game, he seemingly couldn't miss and was "owning the court," dribbling behind his back, between his legs, between opposing players' legs, juking here, faking there, and twisting in for close-range scores. Though the team was far in the lead, the coach had seen enough of this style of play and called a time-out. The young players gathered around the coach for his words of wisdom. All in the gym could clearly hear him angrily say to my brother, "Stop with this jungle play! We are not niggers from Chicago!"

Indeed, Black Chicago was always held in mystique to us as the anti, nether region, the symbol of what we were not and what was wrong with our country. What was wrong with our country were the Evanses and the McFaddens. We didn't know them or anything about their lives, but that didn't matter. Because they were Black and lived in Black Chicago, they were, by their very existence, what we were not to be. I was even told—and this is an example of the most extreme type of nonsensical arguments we would hear and accept without questions—never to get in a swimming pool with African Americans because they are slimy and oily, which flows off their bodies into the water and onto our bodies, making us sick, but much worse, it might make us Black.

Now these prejudices—twisted as they were but held as common-sense truth—coincided with a highly religious people. We will unpack how these can go together a bit later in the chapter, but let me share for now about my own spiritual journey and the town in which I was most formed.

Unlike Michael and David, the church was not central to my life, in part because it was so integrated into the culture of our town (at the pleading of my brother and me, we moved into town when I was in eighth grade, so we could more easily see our friends and get around without needing our parents to drive us). With no Catholic church anywhere to be found, my mother pretty much dropped out of attending church. My father, raised Lutheran, would about once a month bring us to the Lutheran church in town. My parents would bring us to Vacation Bible School for one week each summer, and they ensured we attended Confirmation class each week for two years until we were confirmed. Our town was strongly shaped by pietistic Protestant Christianity. We were a dry town (no alcohol was allowed to be sold), our public school would release kids in Confirmation classes early on Wednesday afternoons to attend their church Confirmation training, and no public events were held on Wednesday evenings (Wednesday night was for church activities) or Sundays (which were for Sunday school, church, Sunday evening church, and family and friend visitations), and "missionary youth workers" were allowed in our public schools to visit the students.

Our main youth worker for much of my junior and senior high school years was a young man named Scott Anderson. We would regularly see him at our school, and he could be found at lunchtime sitting at the lunch tables talking with students. He ran our local area Campus Life program, which held events like "Burger Bashes" (free hamburgers!) and Bible studies.

It was the free hamburgers that first drew me in. Then it was the girls. But I soon became more and more curious about the Bible and the Christian life. Halfway through my junior year of high school, Scott Anderson took me out to our local restaurant, the Norseman, and shared the gospel with me. He asked if I wanted to become a Christian. I did indeed and prayed the prayer of confession.

Part 1. Telling the Stories amid National and Local Realities

My life changed substantially from that point. Other Christians—students, teachers, neighbors, and adults at the local churches—all supported my growth in one way or another. Two of my teachers—Lyle and Sandy Heinitz, strong Christians who lived across the street from me—were highly influential. Lyle Heinitz, in fact, eventually left teaching to become a pastor. Christian friends shared with me cassette tapes of Christian bands. The music and words were mind-blowing to me. I learned my early theology from wearing out the tapes while listening to these groups. My basketball coach and teacher—Mr. Sanborn—was a highly committed Christian who counseled me in Christian living over several years. I still have the flashcards with Bible verses he gave me to use in prayer and memorization. He would lead our team in prayer before every game. Several of my "jock" friends were or became Christian when I did, and we spent immense amounts of time together. We supported one another in living pious lives—no messing around with girls, no drinking, smoking, or drugs, no swearing, and attempting to share Christ in how we lived and what we had to say. Adult church members took us on camping trips in the woods of northern Minnesota, teaching us about God during the whole trip while also teaching us how to fish, row a boat, and set up a camp. Scott Anderson mentored all of us through Bible studies, encouraging us to be in church regularly and being there for counsel and support. One of the new Christian classmates I was closest to during this time remains my closest friend to this day. As we often say, we are much more like brothers than friends, just as is the case for Michael and David.

Reflection on Our Growing-Up Years

Several sociological truisms can be gleaned from our specific stories of growing up and reaching high school graduation. When we say "sociological," we mean the patterns that go beyond our individual experiences. If someone likes to wear bell-bottom pants, it is an individual choice, and we view most of what we do and believe as exactly that: our choices and preferences. But when we see millions of people of particular ages in a particular nation make the same choice in the same time period, when they didn't make such choices before or after that period, we have to ask: Why, in the 1970s in the United States, did so many (mostly young) people like to wear bell-bottom pants?

Boys to Men and Getting Saved

We will not find the answer by focusing on individual choice. We will not find the answer by trying to explain each person's preference. We will not even find the answer by asking people themselves why they do or do not like bell-bottom pants. The reason is that sociological forces deeply influence those choices and preferences. In the example of the bell-bottom pants, the choices were dramatically influenced by the fashion industry, advertising, popular movies and television shows of the time, one's age, and one's friends. All of those converged to make some choices seem more "right," "in," or even "me."

A famous sociologist back in the 1950s and 1960s, C. Wright Mills, called on us to develop a sociological imagination if we were ever to address social issues.[1] As he illustrated it, if I am poor or rich, and almost no one else in my society is, we need to look at my personal characteristics and decisions to understand why I am poor or rich. But if, say, 25 percent of people in my nation are poor or rich, we need to look at the issue not individually but socially. There is, in fact, something about the nation itself that a quarter of all its people are poor or rich. Perhaps its economic system does not produce enough jobs. Perhaps the economic system has an amazing way of supporting and rewarding entrepreneurship that generates a far-above-average business-start-up success rate. Regardless of the reason, studying each individual to learn why they are poor or wealthy misses the point. As C. Wright Mills noted, in such cases we must understand the society in which people live, and we must understand *the historical moment in which the society finds itself*.

Anyone reading this book who is younger than this book's authors likely grasps the latter. Our growing up in the 1960s and 1970s into the early 1980s is, to them, history, a history younger readers recognize as such because it was "before their time." They can, therefore, easily account for our personal stories as a product of the historical moment in which we were raised. They may not so easily identify, however, the impacts of the society itself.

But anyone reading this book who is from a different society surely can. They may have thought to themselves a time or two while reading this chapter, "How peculiarly American," or "That is surely different than in my country." And this reality points to a key building block for ultimately achieving kingdom racial change. Every single one of us oc-

---

1. C. Wright Mills, *The Sociological Imagination* (New York: Oxford University Press, 1959).

Part 1. Telling the Stories amid National and Local Realities

cupies *a social location*—a specific place in the social world within a specific society within a specific historical moment. We thus assess the world and suggest how it should be improved from our social location, what we know to be true (Building Block 2).

Our stories illustrate in bold relief that, although Rev. Ev., David, and Michael occupy the same society in the same historical moments, we occupy vastly different social locations within an unequal and segregated society. Those social locations led our parents and us to make different decisions than we would if we occupied an alternative social location. Our unique social locations led us to encounter unique situations, to address our situations with the resources available to us, and to perceive and relate to the world in different ways.

Let us break down these sociological truisms into two categories: what we can call white advantage and Black advantage. Of course, if we had different racial or ethnic backgrounds, our analysis would be different. But since the authors are Black or white, we shall focus on these social locations.

Emerson had many, many economic and personal advantages growing up. On his father's side, his great-great-grandparents emigrated from Norway and, being perceived as white immediately, were able to settle in the upper Midwest, access land, and farm for several generations until his father's generation, which was the first to go to college.

Why were Emerson's father and many of his peers able to go to college then? Emerson's father and most of his father's male siblings joined the military. They were given funding for their service to attend college (his father's two sisters, not able to access such benefits, did not attend college). Colloquially known as the "GI Bill," the act provided returning servicemen with, among other benefits, funds for education. This bill allowed, for the first time, significant numbers of nonelites to attend college. Emerson's father and his brothers did not go to "prestigious" colleges. Still, they went at a time (mostly the 1950s) when not many people graduated from college and when many persons of color were barred from or greatly discouraged from attending most colleges, universities, and trade schools. They also went at a time when the economy was changing, requiring more highly educated people to fill the new roles in the soon-to-come "computer age." It was in that time period that Emerson's father entered college, being among the first generation of people to make their living working entirely on computers—programming, analyzing, designing, and improving for greater speed and analysis power.

Boys to Men and Getting Saved

If Emerson's father and siblings could take advantage of their military service to catapult themselves into solid middle-class status, why didn't Rev. Ev.'s and Dr. David's fathers do the same? The simple answer: they were Black.

The GI Bill did not say Black men could not benefit, but it did so in practice. One way this was done was by the lawmakers' deal to have this federal program be administered by each individual state, allowing local prejudices to be exercised. From the start of the program, Black veterans found it difficult to access the benefits. Stories of being stonewalled, delayed endlessly, or flat-out denied abound. But if somehow the benefits could be accessed, Black veterans found it even more difficult to find institutions willing to allow them to use those benefits. Black veterans were excluded from many colleges, universities, and trade schools. Having money to pay for an education in such an environment was of no use.

This all had a substantial impact that influenced us as their children and on into the current age. The newly created skilled positions requiring higher education during our fathers' time went overwhelmingly to white men because they ended up being the people with the required education. They were the "best persons" for the jobs because a discriminatory system generated that result. Getting an education with little or no debt and then getting good-paying jobs allowed white men of this era to take advantage of the government's home-financing programs in order to flow out into new suburbs and to amass wealth in their homes and in their professions. Emerson, Evans, and McFadden were all born into this reality; but only Emerson was born into the advantaged side.

Our mothers all lived in a generation with limited educational, occupational, and income opportunities for women during at least the first thirty to forty years of their lives. A main way for advancement was through marriage. Emerson's mother, the daughter of uneducated Italian peasants with limited English skills, grew up working-class within mostly Italian-speaking communities. But being "white" afforded her and her siblings the ability to assimilate within a generation. When Emerson's mother married his father in 1960, it was a big deal for two reasons: ethnicity (Norwegian, Italian) and religion (Protestant, Catholic). But after working through the family issues, upon her marriage she became middle-class because her husband was middle-class. She also became much more assimilated into the larger white society, having married into a family that had been in the United States for multi-

Part 1. Telling the Stories amid National and Local Realities

ple generations. Because of Emerson's father's sufficient income, his mother rarely worked outside the home. During their growing-up years, she was always a stay-at-home mom until his parents purchased a roller rink. But though she worked at the roller rink, that meant only three or four days a week for a few evening and weekend hours, and always with her children working at the roller rink with her.

For the other two authors, their mothers did not become middle-class upon marriage. They had to struggle. Either they had to work while juggling many responsibilities, or if they chose to stay home to raise their children, they did so being poor or, at best, being working-class. Much uncertainty was the result—sometimes having enough, other times having almost no money for essentials.

The sociological imagination allows us to see the many advantages afforded to Emerson that were not possible for Evans or McFadden. What is so difficult to accept in our American culture is that so many of these advantages and disadvantages are not shaped by our individual character, choices, or actions. They are shaped by our social location within a specific society within a specific historical moment.

This, of course, does not mean individual character, choice, and action don't matter; they do. Rather, it means that we are catapulted or constrained in profound ways by social forces beyond our individual character, choices, and actions. To illustrate, if there are only three good-paying jobs in a community of 3,000 adults, then 2,997 people will not have good-paying jobs, no matter how hard they work, no matter how much education they get, and no matter how sacrificial and dedicated they are. The problem is what we call a structural issue—the economy is not producing enough good-paying jobs. It requires, therefore, a social solution. That is, rather than asking people to get yet more education or to work even harder, we need to focus our energy on expanding the number of good-paying jobs.

Here is one more illustration. David McFadden describes often having to spend hours traveling with his brother by city bus to get healthy groceries. Emerson has no such tale to tell. Want good groceries? Walk or hop in the car to the nearest grocery store. All grocery stores in his world had good and healthy food options. Grocery stores were abundant wherever he lived.

David, however, lived in a housing project; he was Black in segregated Chicago and had to leave his community to get healthy food options. So why should the journey take hours? Why did he and his brother often have to wait an hour or more for a bus to come by—and even when it did, it might be so crowded they would have to wait for the next one?

Gwendolyn Purifoye, a professor at Notre Dame, has spent years riding and studying public transportation in Chicago and elsewhere. She documents with visual clarity that a segregated city means more transportation options in the white parts of Chicago and fewer options in Black and Hispanic Chicago. There are more trains and buses covering more ground with less space between stops in white Chicago, with nicer equipment and larger, extended buses serving for more hours than in the rest of Chicago.

David experienced this reality. Residing in Black Chicago's far south side meant no access whatsoever to the city's extensive "L" (elevated) train system (the southbound train's last stop is several miles north of where David lived). It also meant fewer and smaller buses that served fewer stops far less frequently than in white Chicago. Hence, when a bus did come by, it could be after an hour or more wait, and it could be so crowded because everyone was attempting to get where they needed to go in a far-too-limited public-transportation system. And they needed to go somewhere more often because they did not have as many essentials in their neighborhoods—such as grocery stores with healthy food.[2]

In the United States, we are used to hearing about how white folks have advantages over Black folks (even if many of us white folks often deny such advantages can be true). We are not as used to hearing about or understanding the many advantages Black folks have over white folks. Our stories in this chapter, though, clearly illustrate some of those Black advantages. As we work toward kingdom racial change, an important building block is understanding Black advantages just as much as white advantages (Building Block 3).

We can summarize the advantages indicated in this chapter as the three *F*s: family, friends, and faith. Studies repeatedly find that Black Americans have more kin than white folk. Not only that, but studies also find that Black folk are closer to their kin than white folk, as in they spend more time together and more often support one another economically and emotionally. When there are times of trouble, on average,

---

2. See Gwendolyn Purifoye's book, *Race in Motion: Public Transportation and Restricted Mobile Spaces* (New York: NYU Press, 2024), for a much more in-depth analysis and explanation.

Part 1. Telling the Stories amid National and Local Realities

Black Americans have more and deeper family relationships to turn to for support than white Americans. This is partly why we find that Black Americans experience less depression, anxiety, and suicide than white Americans, even though, given life circumstances, we might expect the very opposite. Finally, once we account for differences in education and income—which again are shaped by the larger social forces—studies find that Black fathers are more involved in raising their children than white fathers.

Black Americans have more friends and deeper relationships with their friends than white Americans. As with kin, Black Americans' friendships form a web of support, a network of people in the neighborhood, the larger area, and even in different parts of the country that can and do support one another during challenging times. This is, in part, why, despite all the challenges society insists on casting upon African Americans, African Americans actually report more happiness and positivity toward life than white Americans, especially once we hold constant things like social-class differences.

But perhaps the greatest advantage that Black Americans have is religious faith. Compared to white Americans, Black Americans are much more likely to believe in God, to attend church, to attend church frequently, to pray, to read the Bible, to believe in heaven and hell, and to have a network of fellow believers from whom they gain support and encouragement. Black children and youth, compared to their white counterparts, are less likely to experience religious decline when family disruptions (divorce, death) occur, in part because of the deeper relationships and greater belief and trust in God's providence. Black Americans' religious lives are occupied by a cosmos in which God is more active, powerful, and interested in supporting people than is true within the white religious cosmos. God can and will do anything according to God's will. God never loses battles. God will protect and provide. God is everywhere. Emerson and Jason Shelton wrote an entire book on this very topic called *Blacks and Whites in Christian America*.[3]

The white religious cosmos, in the United States at least, is contorted by a non-Christian intruder, what Emerson and Glenn Bracey call the Religion of Whiteness, which we define as making whiteness (white people and their dominance) sacred and rendering anything that

---

3. Jason Shelton and Michael O. Emerson, *Blacks and Whites in Christian America: How Racial Discrimination Shapes Religious Convictions* (New York: NYU Press, 2012).

does not do this profane.[4] It is a competing religion that distorts white Christianity in many places, churches, and people. See Emerson and Bracey's book *The Religion of Whiteness* for a full explanation. To illustrate, though, recall Emerson describing his religious town as a place where racial prejudice, ignorance, and white superiority effortlessly coexisted with Christianity. It is a deep, long-standing distortion of the Christian faith that is so difficult for most white Christians to see, let alone to disentangle. So most white Christians live in a two-pronged world, where God loves everyone and makes everyone equal, but also where the belief is firmly held that white people are better (or other people fall short). This view is not because white Christian folks view themselves as more committed Christians but because they view themselves as more successful educationally and economically and more dominant culturally. A Black religious advantage is that most of their religious communities have no such twisting of the Christian faith, no need to hold in impossible tension two irreconcilable beliefs—the equality of humanity and white superiority. An important kingdom racial change building block is the urgent and essential need to root out the Religion of Whiteness from religious communities (Building Block 4). Doing so is a fundamental requirement in our path toward God's family.

We see in bold contours all of these advantages playing out in Rev. Ev.'s and David's lives. Despite family disruption and severe challenges, they had deep family relationships and close friendships, and these family and friends played key roles all across their growing-up years, encouraging and supporting them. They had, for example, each other, continuing in friendship to this very day with support, challenge, and encouragement for each other.

The Christian worlds that Rev. Ev. and David grew up in were deep, rich, supportive, educational, aspirational, and transformative. In fact, they both attended a church specifically designed to empower youth such as themselves, encircling them in the Word of God, building them up as Christian leaders, and training them in the disciplines of the faith. The lengths to which their religious communities went to support them are almost stunning. In the face of tremendous challenges and an entire set of social systems working to prevent them from thriving and flourishing, for Rev. Ev. and David the many Black advantages described

---

4. Michael O. Emerson and Glenn E. Bracey II, *The Religion of Whiteness: How Racism Distorts Christian Faith* (New York: Oxford University Press, 2024).

Part 1. Telling the Stories amid National and Local Realities

here worked in conjunction to help each of them resist the lie that they did not matter, that they were inferior, or that they were meant to fail. Family, friends, faith—these three areas of Black advantage are powerful counterweights that lifted, supported, and encouraged Rev. Ev. and David to know their God-given place and worth in the world and to dedicate themselves to God's glory.

3

Getting Down, Getting Out

In this chapter, we track our higher-education years. We can learn much by comparing our experiences as we each attempt to gain the necessary qualifications to pursue dreams and callings and support those around us. We find in comparing our higher-education years that we learn important lessons for kingdom racial change. The key building blocks we arrive at in this chapter are that we must work to create healthy environments starting in childhood (Building Block 5), we need to overcome the unholy link between race and class (Building Block 6), and as Christians we have an amazing opportunity to change the structure of networks and connections (Building Block 7).

Rev. Ev.

The year 1980 was tumultuous for my family and me. I graduated high school and had the opportunity to play baseball for Southern Illinois University. But family events meant I never made it there. Both of my parents—good, dedicated, hard workers—were laid off from their jobs. My parents both worked in major companies. My father worked at Prince Spaghetti as a machine mechanic. My mother worked at Johnson & Johnson Company on the west side of Chicago. She was a line inspector who made sure the right numbers of the products were in packages and that they were closed properly. She was moved around from station to station daily. Her factory turned out medical supplies and various cosmetic items. She was laid off like many others for the downturn in retail sales of their products and the eventual closing of the factory.

My father, being a machine mechanic, was typically able to get work. His motto was all machines are similar. If you can fix one, you can fix

Part 1. Telling the Stories amid National and Local Realities

them all. For him, that worked just fine; he was a quick study, and he was good at anything he put his mind to. He very much liked working at Prince Spaghetti. So when he was laid off in August 1980, for the first time I could remember, he felt very bad about losing that job. He knew it would not be as easy as it was for him in the past to find good-paying work. The world was a different place now. Most of the good-paying jobs had moved to distant suburbs, moved overseas, or just closed. Time was tough all around in the city, and his impressive skills couldn't open doors like they used to. He would never get another job he liked as much or that paid as well. The deindustrialization of the economy pounded my parents economically because as the economy changed to be more information-based, they lacked the education and networks to move into the newly created jobs that were replacing the factories.

My parents were eventually able to find new jobs, but at substantially reduced pay rates. Even with their combined income, they simply could not make the payments on our house. In short order, in November 1980, our house was foreclosed—disruption in our family life once again. All of us were deflated and devastated. We were working hard yet going backward.

So allow me to back up just a bit. I had graduated high school back in May. I had the opportunity to go to Southern Illinois University to play baseball there. But with what was occurring in my family—the instability and economic insecurity—I passed on that possibility. My thought was I needed to make money to help the family. David, not opposed to that thought, wanted me to get an education too. He strongly encouraged me to apply and enroll at Chicago State (a primarily Black university on Chicago's south side, where he was attending). Convinced, I enrolled just a week before the fall semester began and was able to play baseball for the university.

But I still had to work to try to help my family. I started working at Jewel food store, and a couple of months later—through the help of a fellow church member—I added a second job at UPS, working 10 p.m. to 2 a.m. I was killing myself. I was working at UPS at night, getting off at 2:00 in the morning, commuting home, getting to bed around 3 a.m., getting up a few hours later to go to school from 8 a.m. to 12 p.m. during the day, and playing baseball after my last classes daily, getting a little rest, then going to work at UPS from 10 p.m. to 2 a.m. And on weekends and holidays, I worked at the grocery store as a bagboy and then as a cashier. The word *tired* could not express how I felt. Nor could it capture the disappointment I had for myself for the many times I was late for my 8 a.m. first class.

To be honest, I was frustrated at what was going on. My family needed my help, as my big brother had already gone to the Army. Other than paying my tithes and for bus fare and a few things I might need to buy, I gave the rest of my money from both jobs to my parents, trying to help save our home. Yet, no matter how hard I worked, it was not enough. We still lost our house.

To make matters worse, I was experiencing real difficulties at work, especially at my UPS job. At UPS, I was a truck unloader. I didn't have to be a genius to figure out how to do that job, right? Wrong. I was threatened almost every other night to be fired! Never had a boss or supervisor spent his time cursing and hollering at me for poor performance before. But yes, this eighteen-year-old athlete couldn't keep up. I wanted to make something out of the fact that my super was white, five foot five, but he was right. I was late every day, and I was the slowest person on my shift.

There was a good reason I was late so often. My shift started at 10 p.m. After coming home from baseball, getting something to eat, and taking a short nap if I could, I would head to the bus stop to catch the bus that went closest to where I worked. Based on the bus schedule, I would arrive at State and Roosevelt (what is today called the South Loop, where highly educated, white-collar people live) at 9:45 p.m., with more than enough time for me to jog the mile from the bus stop down to Roosevelt and Canal Street at the UPS entrance in seven to eight minutes. I had time to spare. Young and in shape, the jog was no problem. Except for one thing: I am Black.

A young Black man running in a high-rent district near downtown, it turns out, is perceived as a serious problem by others. Nearly every night, I would get stopped by the police, shoved up against a wall, and told to spread! They detained me even though I would tell them I worked at UPS and was jogging so I would not be late. When I reached for my ID, their guns were immediately drawn, and fear of death gripped my heart most nights. No matter what I said, the same thing would happen night after night. The police would hold me for between seven and ten minutes, making it impossible for me to be on time. When the police would let me go, I still had about two or three minutes to be on time, but now I feared if I started running to work again, the police would say I was running from them and I would get a bullet in the back of my

Part 1. Telling the Stories amid National and Local Realities

head. So I would just walk as quickly as I could until they drove around the corner, and then I would sprint like I was trying to steal second base. Because I was fast, I was never grossly late, but still three or four minutes late each night. This perpetual few minutes late to my shift enraged my supervisor, so he was mad before I even touched a box. That rage grew because, in his words, I was the slowest on the line. Then came the threats to be fired nightly.

I repeatedly tried to explain how the police would stop me every night on my way to work. But he would say, "Do the police hold your arms in the trucks and make you my slowest man on the line!" I was caught in a no-win situation.

Despite my nightly troubles with the police, there was something that greatly disturbed me. Why was the person in the best physical shape of his life the slowest person in this job? I could barely finish a truck and a half, despite working as hard and as fast as I could, and the quota was two trucks per night. I was puzzled and troubled.

But first things first. I had to stop being detained by the police. So, the next time they stopped me, I would try something bold and pray my life would not be the cost of it. When the police stopped me like always, I let them grab my ID, which I now kept clipped to my coat collar. I said to them, "Excuse me, officers, could you give me a letter or note for my supervisor who's going to fire me for being late every night?"

The first time, they pushed me in the back and said, "Are you trying to get smart with us?"

"Oh, no, sirs. I just need my job."

"Keep moving," is what they told me.

That was the shortest time I was delayed. I did not get a note, but I had enough time to make it to work before my shift started. My new strategy seemed to work.

Now, I had to fix why I was the slowest unloader in the building. After the super hollered yet again and threatened to fire me, he left for a while. I got out of my truck and went over to the only female who worked my shift to see how in the world a much smaller person could be able to do this job better than I could.

I watched her work for ten to twelve minutes. I found she wasn't faster or stronger, just smarter. She would pull the box conveyor belt into her truck as close to the boxes as she could. Instead of reaching for each box as we were taught, she carefully started a controlled box avalanche, having the boxes fall onto the conveyer belt. She then pushed them out of the truck as neatly as she could. The box avalanche she started would let the box conveyor belt do most of the work. UPS taught us to handle one box at a time so we wouldn't break anything, but I learned that method was doomed to failure. The controlled-avalanche method was ingenious and inspiring and did not harm the boxes' contents.

Even though now I had not been unloading my truck for nearly fifteen minutes, with this new method, I was able for the first time to get two trucks unloaded as fast as the next person. By week's end, I was the fastest guy on the line. I was the fastest guy in the building in less than a month, regularly unloading four or more trucks per night.

Now the problem was I was too good at my job. Other workers got mad at me for going so fast. But I got promoted to the sorter's position with a seventy-five-cent pay raise per hour.

As far as the police, my new method was helpful. The next time they saw me running to work, I heard only a brief sound of their siren. Then I heard them saying as they drove by, "That's the same nigger. Just let him go." No more getting stopped, but still no respect.

Despite my working two jobs and all the variety of jobs my father and mother could find, as I noted above, we lost our home. We were back on the move again. We found a house to rent and would be there for approximately eighteen months. The house was owned by a fireman, Clint Maxwell, whose fire station was down the street. My parents, struggling to get gainful employment that paid more than minimum wage, would often be late on the rent.

That angered Clint Maxwell, who lived in the basement of the house. One tactic he would use to create fear in my family and show he was mad would be to let his three wild and loud-barking Doberman Pinschers run around in the backyard. Sometimes, he would throw one large piece of meat out in the yard so they would fight over it. This was his way of showing how mad he was when the rent was late.

The last straw came when the rent was only partially paid, and he went out in the yard and shot his gun up in the air two times. He would repeat the gesture when David Evans, my father, only gave him $100 more. This was Clint's way of saying, "I want all my money now."

That same day, my father borrowed $400 from two of his sisters and a friend, not to pay the rent but to rent a U-Haul truck. While Clint was at the fire station for one of his twenty-four-hour shifts, we packed the U-Haul truck, moving out all our belongings at night. We once again moved to

Part 1. Telling the Stories amid National and Local Realities

my father's sister Clara's apartment in the Englewood neighborhood, as we had done sixteen years earlier when we first arrived in Chicago.

By 1983—when I was a junior at Chicago State—my parents were laid off from the underpaying jobs they had secured when they were laid off three years earlier. This time around, it was worse. My mother could not find a new job. My father did not fare well either. He bounced around, working wherever he could just to keep the rent and bills paid. It was clear to me: I needed to do more to help the family. And doing so most certainly altered my future.

Though I greatly enjoyed playing baseball for Chicago State, I made the decision to quit the team and take on additional work. It still wasn't enough. Our family was bouncing around from place to place, living with relatives and friends, a few weeks here, a few weeks there. Life was completely unstable and uncertain.

So later that year, I made an even bigger decision. Despite being part of an incredible college ministry with David and others and despite recognizing the importance of a college degree, I dropped out of college altogether to work full-time. My dear friend David tried to convince me not to take the route of leaving school. But in my heart, I knew I had to help my family. They needed the money to stay afloat. With such tenuous employment, we often existed without health-care coverage, and bills could pile up quickly. My full-time employment was comprised of working several jobs at once—in addition to the ones I have already mentioned, I worked some combination of positions at Burns Security Company, Sandwich Chef, a telemarketing firm, and more. I didn't make much, but I did what I could do. What it meant is that I was never able to return to school.

Dr. David

During high school, I initially felt God wanted me to play basketball in the NBA. I went to Ray Meyer's (legendary head coach at DePaul) basketball camp prior to my senior year in high school. I was thrilled when I won the one-on-one competition and was offered a basketball tryout at DePaul after I graduated from high school. I was eager to attend the tryout and had a year to prepare.

However, to play at DePaul, I first had to be accepted into the university. I was not accepted at DePaul because of my low score on the ACT, their required standardized college entrance exam. I was devastated. My dream of playing for DePaul for a chance at the NBA was over in a flash, as I did not qualify academically.

Like so many Black youth, I never tested well on standardized tests. It was bewildering to me, as I loved my classes and did well in school. In grade school, I was exceptional in math. It came easy. It was like playing a game. In junior high, noticing that my vocabulary was limited, I forced myself to read a variety of books to build my vocabulary. I have continued to read ever since.

I was always near the top of my class in both grade school and high school. I was one of the few to take the highest math course offered at my high school during my senior year. But when I took the ACT (twice), I floundered both times. I was deeply discouraged and truly wondered if I would ever go to college. I did not even want to apply. It seemed it was not for me.

Though basketball was over for me, I knew I needed to attend college. I knew this because our church emphasized the importance of attaining a higher education. Our church leaders constantly preached to us that our ticket out of the projects was an education. I had to draw from my relationship with Christ and my church community to overcome the inferior feeling that I faced due to low standardized-test scores. Although I was not accepted at DePaul, I eventually applied and was accepted at the University of Illinois Chicago and Chicago State University. I chose Chicago State University because my brother and a church friend attended there. All of us were able to afford the cost because, at least during Jimmy Carter's tenure as president of the United States, we were able to receive government grants to cover our tuition. We lived at home and commuted back and forth to class.

Attending Chicago State, a primarily Black university, was a very good decision because I excelled academically and thrived in my social and spiritual life. Michael Evans and another close friend, John, joined me, and we headed Christian Fellowship, a campus Christian youth organization. This is when my relationship with Michael and John truly deepened. We were inseparable. They called us the three amigos.

Christian Fellowship provided a platform to develop both our teaching and our leadership skills. We taught lessons on a rotating weekly schedule. We were radical in our approach to galvanizing the Christian student body at Chicago State. I must say that Christian Fellowship was the highlight of my college experience. Michael and I would later use

Part 1. Telling the Stories amid National and Local Realities

what we learned at Christian Fellowship and apply it as adults to our men's racial unity group.

My other main task at Chicago State was to prepare for and enter medical school. As God will do, he used my disappointment in my basketball dreams to instill a different dream, one God has made clear to me was my life's calling. My aspirations shifted from hoop dreams to becoming a physician. I could not stop thinking about it. There were and are far too few African American physicians. I wanted to help change that.

Chicago State isn't a highly ranked university, but it has prepared many of the Black physicians that we have in our country today. The Black student body and instructors at Chicago State provided an incubator that unleashed the confidence I needed to prepare for the arduous, grueling journey to enter medical school.

Medical school required applicants to have good grades and high scores on the medical-school standardized exam, the MCAT, to be accepted. During college at Chicago State, I made the dean's list multiple times and had a high GPA despite taking many rigorous math and science courses.

But once again, the standardized test loomed. My fears and doubts weighed in on me. As before, I did not do well on the standardized test. I felt horrible after receiving my scores. I felt insufficient, like an imposter. I wanted to give up.

But a friend who attended Chicago State University and my church, Bobby Scales, greatly encouraged me. He had been accepted into medical school three years before, and he kept me focused on applying despite my MCAT score.

With his encouragement and support, I went ahead and applied. It did not go well. I received just one interview but was turned down due to racial issues. Let me explain. During the interviewing process for this medical school, a professor was clearly biased against my admission. He did not want a Black student from a lowly ranked university to harm the medical school's image. This led to my being denied admission.

I was devastated and heartbroken, and my confidence again was shattered. I had mustered whatever courage I could find to apply, but the end result was the same—I was not good enough. My experience is far too common. Many Black people encounter multiple obstacles in their attempt to follow the American path—work hard and "succeed." What ultimately then happens is severe discouragement and abandonment of their dreams and goals. Dreams are not deferred but instead crushed. Along with that, one's confidence and direction are gone. For so many African Americans, low test scores lead to an inferiority complex, then hopelessness with no real tangible way out of the hood. So many young men subsequently give their lives to violence and crime due to low self-esteem.

Devastated and dejected as I was, my support network would not let me quit. My church would not let me quit. God would not give me peace until I tried again. I was counseled to enroll in a graduate program in biology at Chicago State for a year and then reapply, taking the time to bone up on MCAT exam preparation. So I did exactly that, and upon retaking the MCAT, my score, though not outstanding, did improve. I then applied again to medical schools. To my encouragement, it went better. I was accepted into three programs. I chose the medical school I did both because it was the first to accept me and because it was in my home state.

But sadly, it wasn't peaches and roses from there. Quite the opposite. Truth be told, the next chapter in my life was the worst of my existence. My experience of medical school was brutal, repeatedly depressing, and downright racist. I never knew how Black I was until I entered medical school. What usually takes four years to complete took me five-and-a-half grueling, painful, and too-often humiliating years to complete.

Why? I faced repeated, superfluous racial hurdles that I was made to cross, hurdles that were nonexistent for my white counterparts. This was my first entry into a primarily white world, and never had I experienced such intense racism on this level in my life. Institutionalized racism is probably more harmful than outright, blatant, in-your-face racism. You cannot tell from which direction it is coming or when it will hit. Every day, I had to watch my back academically. I came to understand that in each and every course I must make sure that at least one white student had lower grades than me to avoid dismissal.

One of my first classes was pathology. I remember entering the class and the instructor staring at me as though I didn't belong. Her disdain for my presence was painfully obvious. It became clear to me that I would have to battle every day not to get dismissed. One of the Black students I started with—there were eleven of us—was dismissed after the first year of the program. Not too long after that, another Black student was dismissed. We were down to nine of us. We were all walking on eggshells.

Part 1. Telling the Stories amid National and Local Realities

I used all the godly tools I had acquired to survive. I prayed. I often studied in the wee hours of the night to stay afloat. I developed relationships with the local church and became good friends with some of the men at the church. One of the men, James Davis, and I developed a strong bond that offered a source of encouragement I sorely needed. His family often provided much-needed meals during my time in medical school. The remaining Black students and I formed a study group. This provided comradery and support and helped us all in our studies.

But the road continued to be rocky. Medical-school students use previous exams to study for upcoming tests. But whereas the Black students were able to get access to about ten prior tests, the white students were working with many previous exams, a clear advantage for them. They had access to more exams because they had much better and closer relationships with our (white) professors. Not infrequently, in fact, they would have dinner together at the professors' homes, something that almost never occurred for the Black students.

During my third year, my clinical year, I ran into trouble. One of my first clinical classes or clerkships was obstetrics and gynecology. This clerkship was exciting because I found much joy in safely delivering babies. During our clerkship, a major component of the grade was subjective. You could fail the clerkship if your instructor didn't feel you performed adequately clinically. There were no clear guidelines. It was simply up to the professor's "professional judgment." This was a problem because no matter how hard you might work, if your instructor wasn't happy with your performance or didn't like you, you could fail the clerkship, no questions asked.

During the early part of the OB/GYN clerkship, I knew I wasn't doing well because my instructor said so. To try to improve my grade, I worked harder and even stayed over the Thanksgiving holiday to put in extra time to improve my grade. This was to no avail. I was given a failing grade.

I was devastated. There it was again—the clear thought and communication that I, as a person, was insufficient and defective, something hard work didn't seem to overcome. I was so utterly discouraged, and my confidence was so thoroughly shaken, that it led to poor performance in my next clerkship—surgery—and so I also failed that clerkship. At this point, I knew I was in serious jeopardy of being dismissed.

Just as I thought, I was informed that a dismissal hearing was scheduled for me. I was horrified, desperate, and did not know where to turn for help. I fell to my knees and cried out to Christ for help. I began to prepare my defense against dismissal. I approached some of the faculty for support. To my surprise, I received strong support letters from a couple of faculty members stating that I was a very good student. At this point, I was confused as to why I was receiving failing grades when at least some of the faculty felt I was doing well.

Desperate, I went to the local National Association for the Advancement of Colored People (NAACP). The organization would prove to be instrumental during my dismissal hearing. They provided me with a local attorney who worked on civil-rights issues. I was poor and had no money to pay the attorney. He took my case pro bono. The attorney helped me prepare the case extremely well. During the beginning of the dismissal hearing, my attorney represented me in a way I could never have done on my own.

The members of the dismissal hearing were shocked that I brought an attorney because they knew I had no money. They delayed the hearing for about an hour to huddle. They recognized that they would not be able to railroad me, and they were now concerned about the civil-rights ramifications. My attorney and I presented a strong case, and I was not dismissed. What a relief (which is an understatement).

The relief was short-lived. Although I was allowed to continue my medical education, the troubled waters did not abate. A board exam was given after my second year and, faced with yet another standardized test, I did not do well. The exam was not required by our medical school to graduate, however. We could take a similar exam during our internship, which I did, and I was able to pass it.

But because I didn't do well on the board exam, my medical school required me to take a reading test to determine if I could comprehend what I read. How humiliating and demeaning. I was a college graduate, yet they were making me take a test to see if I could read and understand. Even more, I soon learned that the dean of the medical school did not think I could graduate. He was actually betting against me. I took their reading test and showed that I clearly could read and comprehend the material.

I returned to my clerkship and was successful in getting through. I finally could see the light at the end of the medical-school tunnel. One of my last clerkships was in pediatrics. Again, I had trouble on the exam and failed the final. As a result, still another dismissal hearing was scheduled.

Part 1. Telling the Stories amid National and Local Realities

Again, I had to fight off thoughts that I didn't belong. Through Jesus, I mustered enough strength to fight back. Like so many other Black students, I was completely discouraged and humiliated. And like so many Black students, I wanted to drop out. I had been told repeatedly that I was insufficient. I was on a razor's edge, so close to giving in to others' assessment of my insufficiencies. I would often call my mother in the midnight hour to pour out my heart and ask for prayer. My two best friends, Michael and John, were often needed to keep me mentally and spiritually from falling apart. This kept me from falling into the abyss of "not good enough."

Also during this time, I met my future wife, Tanya, at a Christian party. My relationship with her was another main reason I made it through medical school (God provides!). She believed in me, and she encouraged me. It went even further. Finances were always a struggle, as I had almost no time to work and could not rely on family for help, struggling as they were themselves. One day I came home from class only to find my furniture on the lawn. I was evicted due to unpaid rent and was suddenly homeless. Godsends, Tanya and her family took me into their home, where I stayed in the basement. One night, while in the basement of their home, I heard the voice of God saying that I would make it through medical school. Without a shadow of a doubt, I knew this was God. This gave me hope to fight on.

What I discovered in preparation for the second dismissal hearing, with the help of my attorney, was that other students had failed the test but were given another opportunity to take the exam. I was not given this opportunity. When presenting this information to the dismissal committee, which they already knew but were not going to share with me, they then gave me a chance to retake the exam. I passed.

And with that, after five-and-a-half painful years, I was finally allowed to graduate from medical school. I was so angry at how I had been treated during medical school that I didn't attend the graduation ceremony.

After completing an internal medicine residency, I was accepted at the University of Alabama's nephrology program. I was the second Black person accepted into the program. At that time, the chairman of nephrology was searching for Black candidates for an important reason. He knew that although over 35 percent of patients on dialysis were Black, only 4 percent of nephrologists were Black, which was far too large of a disparity.

During my nephrology fellowship, my chairman would often have me speak at Black churches about hypertension and kidney disease. I was essentially the medical ambassador to the Black community in Birmingham. So, unlike my time in medical school, my time in Birmingham, Alabama, was fulfilling and exhilarating. I was wanted and empowered, and I thrived in helping others. In fact, at the time of completing the fellowship, neither my wife, Tanya, nor I wanted to leave.

But we had to go back home to Chicago to care for my mother. So we moved back to my home city, where I practiced as a full-fledged medical doctor. We eventually built a home. At thirty-four years of age, this was the first home in which I had ever lived. To our pure joy, my wife and I later built my mother a home down the street from where we lived. What an honor and privilege it was for me to provide this home for my mom after all the sacrifices she made for me.

Michael Emerson

As I moved toward graduating high school, I knew I would go to college. I was not, however, in a hurry to attend, because I was not certain what I wanted to study. Somewhere along the way, I decided to wait. I first explored enlisting in the military, so my dad and I had recruiters come to our house to learn about the different branches. But God said no to that route. It just did not seem a fit, and my father agreed.

At that point, I had what, in retrospect, was a somewhat crazy idea. A few years earlier, my family had taken a vacation to Disneyland in California. My idea was that I would move by myself to Southern California and find a job, ideally at Disneyland itself. Somehow, I convinced my parents to let me do this.

The plan was simple. I had some Italian relatives who lived in the LA area. I would fly to the airport nearest them, they would pick me up, and I would stay with them until I found work and could get a place of my own.

My destination was the home of my Aunt MaryAnn and her family. My aunt was a close childhood friend and first cousin of my mother. She, in fact, looked and acted like my mother. A few decades earlier, she had made the same trek as me, from Minnesota to Southern California. She met a Mexican man, married, and now they lived in an LA suburb with their two young teenage daughters. Because of her children's

Part 1. Telling the Stories amid National and Local Realities

ages and gender, she and her husband welcomed me but not into their home. Instead, I slept in a camper in their driveway.

Not college-educated, Aunt MaryAnn had started as a bank teller for a California bank and risen up to an assistant bank manager (and, soon thereafter, branch manager). She was able to get me a position at her bank branch as a teller. I was glad for the position, and after a time there, I wanted to skip college and instead work my way up the bank hierarchy like my aunt had done. I got myself a studio apartment across the street from my bank branch, allowing me to easily get to and from work, showing my commitment.

But that dream ended about nine months later when I was assigned to help a recent UCLA graduate learn the banking basics. Only after a few weeks of teaching him did I discover that, in another two weeks, he would become my boss because he was a college graduate, and I was not. I also learned that although I could rise up the ranks of tellers through study and passing tests, I could not rise to the management position at which this recent college grad was starting, because I did not have a college degree. Clearly times had changed since my aunt could progress through the ranks with only a high school diploma. I would indeed need to go to college.

I was back to my original plan of a single gap year and thus began applying to universities. During that time, though, I was desperate to visit Disneyland. I could never go because when the buses to Disneyland ran from where I lived, I was working. On weekends, when I could go, no buses ran the route I needed. I did not have nearly enough money to take a taxi, and my relatives were unable to take me.

I could stand it no more. So I took a day off during the week—unpaid—and went to Disneyland. I was so excited. But it was here that I learned a deep sociological truth, a truth about how God has created us. I went on ride after ride, going on my favorite rides multiple times. But it wasn't fun. First, it was embarrassing. At least at that time, people didn't go to Disneyland alone. So when I got on rides, I often held up the process because the operator attempted to find someone else to fill the seat next to me. Then, even more importantly, after a ride was completed, there was no one I knew with whom to share the experience of the ride. Whereas we usually would excitedly talk about it with our friends or family, I simply got off and moved on. So I learned a truism: meaning and enjoyment come from sharing experiences with others. The exact same activities done alone are hollow.

My gap year came to an end, and I moved back home with my parents in Minnesota. Little did I know that my mother and one of her friends—the mother of a young lady named Joni—had determined we would make a perfect pair and plotted to get us together. I will spare the details, but it worked. Upon returning home, I started dating Joni. We fairly quickly realized we were meant for each other, and we were married between my sophomore and junior years of college. This is why we both say our marriage was arranged. It truly was.

After much exploration, I determined to attend Loyola University of Chicago, as I wanted to be in a large city for my college years. I applied and was accepted, but because I applied so late in the application cycle, Loyola told me to attend a community college for a year and then reapply to get scholarships.

So that I did. I attended Minneapolis Community College for a year, taking general classes. My grandmother got me a job at the Italian restaurant where she waitressed, as it was near my school. My earnings as a busboy and dishwasher and at a second job cleaning a building a few times a week (usually midnight to 2 a.m.) were sufficient to cover the costs of my tuition. My parents paid for my living expenses. I truly loved learning and eagerly went to class each day. The professors were supportive and, seeing how eager I was to learn, often invited me to talk with them or to connect me with others studying specific topics in which I was interested.

The following year, I did indeed transition to Loyola. Because I scored highly on the required standardized test (at that time, the ACT), I was offered a generous scholarship, which paid for nearly all of my tuition and fees.

Courses at Loyola were at another level of intensity, and I loved them all the more. Because it is a Catholic school, I was required to take several theology courses in addition to a broad spectrum of other courses. I was introduced to the tradition of Catholic social justice and participated in Loyola-sponsored volunteering, such as working at soup kitchens, providing meals and blankets to the homeless, and advocating for better policies to improve the lives of poor families and homeless persons. I was mentored by several clergy—brothers and priests—on campus, helping me situate my studies within the larger context of serving God and serving others.

My lay professors, too, were amazingly supportive. They offered me many opportunities to learn more outside of the classroom, spent time

Part 1. Telling the Stories amid National and Local Realities

talking with me in their offices, and connected me to scholars working in areas in which I was most interested. They encouraged me every step of the way.

When I became a sociology major, a young professor who specialized in the study of religion was our sociology club advisor. He was incredibly generous with his time and was a fast-rising star in the field. He was supportive of my studies, and we remain colleagues to this day, as we both work in the study of religion. Another one of my professors saw my strong interest in all things urban. Her husband was a professor of urban sociology at the University of Chicago. She arranged for me to be his research assistant on a book he was writing about Chicago. I learned an amazing amount from him, not only about urban sociology but about how research is done. In being invited to their home many times, I also observed how they lived the lives of professors, writing, thinking, researching, and teaching.

When I took the urban sociology course offered at Loyola, I befriended the professor of the course. He was a high-level demographer, and I spent a good deal of time learning from him data-analysis techniques and how demographics impact cities, religious institutions, families, and so much more. He invited me to take a graduate statistics course he was teaching, even though I was only an undergrad, and he even got me an offer to work for the Nielsen TV rating company.

He had attended graduate school at the University of North Carolina (UNC), a top-five PhD program in sociology. I endeavored to do the same. I took the required standardized test (the Graduate Record Examinations) and placed in the top 10 percent of test takers. But given the competitiveness of the program, my standardized test score and GPA (4.0) were not enough. I would have to come highly recommended by highly regarded people. With my urban demography professor's recommendation (and his phone calls to professors at UNC), along with my recommendations from the professors noted above, I not only was accepted into the program, but I also received free tuition and a generous stipend for living expenses.

Graduate school was intense. I studied all day and several nights, Monday through Saturday, taking Sundays off for church and social time. Again, several professors went above and beyond teaching in the classroom to help me develop as a scholar and to build my social network of scholars. I was invited to many of their homes. One such professor was a Christian man who spent time showing me and a few of my fellow students how to be a Christian in a secular field. Another was the chair of the department and my advisor, who helped me get my first research papers accepted for presentation at national conferences and who, when asked by other chairs of top departments if he had any outstanding students for hire, would tell them about me. He also did something so above and beyond that I still have a difficult time comprehending it.

After my second year of the graduate program—which takes, on average, seven years to complete—Joni and I were expecting our first child. I felt it my responsibility to get work to support our child and Joni. I had earned my master's and was about to enter the PhD phase, but after talking it over with Joni, I decided to stop at the master's. We let our landlord know we would be moving. We soon packed up a trailer with our belongings and set out to return to Minnesota to set up a life there. Because I knew my advisor would try to talk me out of leaving the program, I waited to tell him until we were already packed and leaving. I had earlier made an appointment, so as we set out to drive to Minnesota, we first stopped at UNC so I could meet with my advisor. While Joni waited in the car, I went in to tell my advisor I was leaving and thanked him for his support.

Long story short, about thirty minutes later, I came out and told Joni, "Guess what? Change of plans. We are going to stay and get the PhD." My advisor had made me an offer I couldn't refuse. He said, "You don't want to stop short of your PhD. You were meant for this. What if I told you that you could get your doctorate in one year? Would you stay? Yes, you would. And yes, you can get your doctorate in one year, just as I did." He then outlined the plan. It would be incredibly intense, with no time off but to go to church, working 6 a.m. to midnight. But he would not have me do any work for him. He would have me work full-time on my final classes, dissertation proposal, and dissertation.

And that is exactly what happened. It took me four years to earn an undergraduate degree, two years to earn a master's degree, and one year to earn a doctoral degree. And with my advisor's help, I found myself with multiple professor positions offered to me from around the country. I accepted the offer from our home state, and there Joni and I moved with our newborn child.

Reflection on Our Higher-Education Years

Our process in writing these chapters is important to know. For each chapter in this first portion of the book, we agreed to write about a spe-

Part 1. Telling the Stories amid National and Local Realities

cific time in our lives. In this chapter, for example, we describe our education after high school. Upon agreeing, we then proceeded to write our stories independently. Only when we put our independent writings into chapter form did we see the similarities or differences in our experiences. We continue to be surprised (shocked?) at the depth of our different experiences.

Reflecting on why they are different is essential in identifying the building blocks for kingdom racial change. What do we learn from this chapter?

The first building block for kingdom racial change we see here is that we must work to create healthy environments starting in childhood (Building Block 5). Consider the deep impacts of life instability for Rev. Ev. and Dr. David, as well as life stability for Emerson. Dr. David was able to live at home during his college years. Still, when he had to move several hundred miles to medical school, on top of all the educational and relational challenges he encountered, he had to attempt to afford an apartment. Given the time he needed to devote to studying, he was not able to earn sufficient income and was evicted from his apartment. Evictions are traumatic life disruptors. They leave one homeless, cause instability in sleeping, eating, and self-care, and cause a range of difficult emotions—from anger to embarrassment, inferiority, confusion, and more. Such events make focusing on intense situations such as medical school extremely difficult. Medical school is all-encompassing, requiring a singular focus for one to succeed. To face dramatic events like eviction, ongoing racism, and questioning of one's abilities, as David repeatedly did, is enough to lead someone to drop out or be dismissed from the program. For David, it led to an intense emotional roller coaster, class and clinical failures, multiple dismissal trials, and an additional year and a half of his life to complete medical school. We read of the extraordinary lengths to which he had to go to survive the program. Becoming the successful medical doctor he is today, saving many lives along the way, came more than close to never happening.

For Rev. Ev., life instabilities in his family were so constant and severe that he was never able to complete college. His family's immediate needs for income to make it to the next month were too ever-present. Committed to his family, he had to forgo his own educational and, ultimately, economic advancement for the sake of his loved ones.

None of this was so for Emerson. His family's comfortable middle-class status meant he encountered no undesired disruptions in his educational journey. He also lived in a home, and if he ran into any personal financial issues, his family backstopped him so that he was able to study uninterrupted both in college and in graduate school. Even his professors multiple times supported him in completing his schooling quickly.

Here is the important learning point. So often, we hear that "it is not race; it is class." Such is the accepted folk wisdom. The problem with this view is it makes two false assumptions: (1) that the cause of things such as disruptions is *either* race *or* class, and (2) that race does not influence class. All we have to do to understand why these are false assumptions is go back to chapters 1 and 2. There we see that racial biases—often encoded in laws and policies—have given decades of advantages to white folks (e.g., where they can live, the mortgages they can access, the use of the GI Bill, the schools they can access, the social connections they have to high-positioned people, being always viewed as the norm and standard) that have led to, on average, higher incomes and dramatically greater wealth for white Americans than for others. In the United States, for racial groups, race *leads* to class. We have clear, several-hundred-year-old racial hierarchies of income and wealth, which have been caused by generations of unequal systems (slavery, Jim Crow segregation, white flight, etc.). Rev. Ev.'s and David's families have repeatedly been on the severe short end across generations. Emerson's family has repeatedly been presented with life-advancing opportunities and benefits unavailable to Rev. Ev.'s and David's families. Those advantages led to a much higher economic class for Emerson's family, and that translated into a remarkably smoother and supportive educational path for Emerson. A key kingdom racial change building block, then, is finding a way to overcome the link between race and class (Building Block 6). It is an unbiblical relationship.

Another impact evident from our stories is our performance on standardized tests, tests used for entry into higher education and used especially for entry into elite institutions of higher education, which in turn shape access to elite professional positions. David repeatedly notes the struggles he had with standardized exams. Despite his hard work and high grades, he struggled over and over when he took standardized tests to enter college and medical school and when he took them to pass medical school. His scores kept holding him back, limiting his opportunities and causing delays in his education, which in turn meant lost income and a full assault on his confidence as a capable person.

Part 1. Telling the Stories amid National and Local Realities

Emerson notes no such struggles. In fact, he only notes that he always "did well" on standardized exams, and his high scores helped open doors to excellent universities and scholarships. This subsequently opened doors to strong connections to well-connected people who helped him ultimately become a professor at several highly ranked universities. He was also able to move through the system rapidly, thus moving to early career advancement and increased earning opportunities.

We might be tempted to say Emerson is simply smarter because his test scores were higher. Emerson can assure you he is not smarter than Rev. Ev. and Dr. David; they are both brilliant. Or we might be tempted to conclude that Emerson worked harder to succeed in his education. We can see in our stories that such a conclusion is patently false. All of us worked hard, year after year.

Rather, our stories illustrate a long-standing truism, again connected to our destructive, unequal history by race. When it comes to standardized tests, racial groups continually perform unequally. Consider, for example, the two main standardized tests used in applying to college, the ACT and the SAT. The ACT's highest possible score is 36. Less than 10 percent of test takers score 30 or higher. Generally, for college, one is looking to score 20 or higher. In 2022—the latest year of summary data at the time of this writing—African American, Native American, and Hispanic students all averaged in the 16 to 17 range. In other words, they are not college-ready. For white and Asian students, the national averages were over 21—in other words, college-ready. The same significant gap is found for the other college entrance exam, the SAT. Generally, one looks to score over 1000. African American, Native American, and Hispanic students had average scores in the 900s; white and Asian students all had average scores of about 1100 or higher.[1]

These differences are not innate differences in smartness. We find, instead, an eerie correlation between parents' economic class and their children's scores on standardized tests. Here, then, is another unfortunate "punishment" of our race-class nexus. The engineered association between race and class in the United States produces significant racial gaps in standardized test scores. Because those scores are so often

---

1. See, for example, the summary information at BestColleges.com, such as Jane Nam, "Average ACT Score," Best Colleges, January 17, 2024, https://tinyurl.com/2tub7fa6.

used to determine college admission and funding, we pass on racial inequality from generation to generation. This is not history. This is our present. And unless we disrupt the system somehow, it is guaranteed to be our future. God weeps.

We need to draw attention to one more vital building block from this chapter. Our stories—those of the authors here and of all people reading this book—are not self-made. We rely on others to be raised; we rely on others to help us navigate a confusing, often difficult world. No matter how gifted we are and no matter how hard we work, we need other people, just as other people need us. We were created by God to be communal; that is, we are meant to live in community. In God's design, communities collectively have what is needed for their members to thrive and to know God. But when we twist communities with inequality, as we have in the contemporary world, the tragedy is we rob ourselves of what God has provided, isolating gifts and isolating people. Such is our fallen nature.

A few years ago, a professor named Deirdre Royster wrote a book called *Race and the Invisible Hand*.[2] She wanted to understand the connection between being educationally successful and ultimately being economically successful. The way she did this was brilliant. She selected and carefully studied a racially mixed high school (50 percent Black, 50 percent white) in Baltimore, a vocational high school for males. In selecting a high school for males only, she did not have to worry about how gender might impact the results. And because every student at this vocational high school was there to learn and then go into a trade—such as electric, masonry, and carpentry—she did not have to be concerned by the complexities of vastly differing career goals. What is more, the students essentially all took the same classes from the same teachers.

She randomly selected twenty-five Black students and twenty-five white students from the exact same year in school. She was able to gather mountains of data about their school experiences, grades, class performances, and family life. What is more, she interviewed these fifty men six years after graduation, so she was able to see what their occupational outcomes were leading up to and at that point. She also interviewed their teachers and school administrators for a richer understanding and to understand their perceptions of the students.

---

2. Deirdre A. Royster, *Race and the Invisible Hand: How White Networks Exclude Black Men from Blue-Collar Jobs* (Berkeley: University of California Press, 2003).

Part 1. Telling the Stories amid National and Local Realities

What did she find? Perhaps you can guess. The white men were doing far better occupationally and economically than the Black men. All the white men were working, compared to 83 percent of the Black men. Among those who were working, for every dollar the Black men earned, the white men earned about $1.25. That means if a Black man was earning $50,000, the white man was earning $62,500. In short, it was as if the white men had been given 25 percent higher raises than the Black men.

She found that nineteen of the twenty-five (76 percent) white men were in "good" blue-collar jobs—trades like electrician, mechanic, computer technician, or mason. Just eight of the twenty-five Black men (32 percent) were in good blue-collar jobs. In fact, over the six years since graduation, twenty-four of the twenty-five Black men had or currently worked in blue-collar jobs that are not trades and don't have a clear path to advancement. These were jobs like food-service work, janitorial work, food delivery, stock boy, and cashier.

The pay gap between Black and white men was for the reason that they were in different types of blue-collar jobs with different pay. But why? Professor Royster set out to discover.

She first considered if the men had paid for additional education after high school, thus giving them a leg up in qualifications. She did indeed find this to be true, but in the opposite direction expected: seventeen of the twenty-five Black men (68 percent) had paid to get additional education, compared to just seven (28 percent) of the white men. Digging deeper, though, she discovered that nine of the white men (36 percent) had additional education paid for them *by their employer*. None of the Black men had ever received this. This was curious, but in the end essentially the same number of Black and white men had additional education. So it did not explain the disparities in occupation and income.

She went back to examine their grades and overall performance in high school. She found no discernable differences. How about difference in innate abilities? Measured with IQ tests and the evaluation of their teachers, she found no discernable differences. So perhaps there were differences in motivation and preparedness to work? No discernable differences were discovered. Perhaps their own parents' educational level differed? Here she did find a difference. But because it was the Black parents who had on average more education than the white parents of these men, it could not explain their children's disparities in occupation and income. How about differences in what the teachers thought of the students or in the percentage getting a teacher recommendation? There was no discernable difference here either.

So what was it? What explained the significant differential outcomes? Her discovery is vitally important for us. She found major differences in social networks, both in *who* the men were connected to and in *how* they were connected. The teachers at this high school were mostly white men who themselves worked in the trades they taught in. As Professor Royster interviewed the fifty men, she came to see clear patterns that they did not. The white men kept talking about how their teachers had helped them get into their trade by loaning them tools (a huge advantage for those just starting), by hiring them in their own businesses, and by proactively reaching out to other companies both to identify unadvertised openings and to give them the personal seal of approval to be hired. Their teachers also offered ongoing feedback to help the white men improve in the trade, and several times the white men spoke of their teachers coming to the actual work sites to help them or inviting them to their homes to show them a needed skill. What is more, the white men shared several times that when they ran into issues at work, their teachers intervened on their behalf to smooth things over and even to get them promotions.

The Black men simply didn't talk this way or experience such help. When Professor Royster interviewed the teachers, they spoke as highly of the Black men as the white men. But when she interviewed the Black men, they did not relay any such help from their teachers as the white men had received. The Black men were in essence on their own, attempting to find work alone or with limited help from people other than their teachers. Some used the placement officer at their high school, a Black woman who had never worked in the trades and had very limited connections. Others reached out to Black men they knew in the blue-collar world. Given US history, this method meant they were reaching out to low-placed Black men either not in the good blue-collar trades or, if they were, with almost no influence to help the students secure employment. And this is why all but one of the Black men had or currently ended up working in blue-collar jobs that were not in the trades, earning less money and having less employment stability and less possibility of economic advancement than their white peers.

Truly, then, it is both who you know and how you know them. As Professor Royster concludes, simply knowing the right people is insuf-

Part 1. Telling the Stories amid National and Local Realities

ficient. You also have to share the right sort of bonds (such as race) with the right people that will then influence what those people are willing to do for you. And this is why she concludes that "visible hands reproduce racial inequality—invisibly."[3]

Consider our stories in this chapter. We see Rev. Ev. and Dr. David struggling, and we see them get support from each other and their church families. What we don't see is them talking about all the help they got from professors who could directly support them in their education and occupational goals. Emerson's story is over and over about well-placed relatives and professors encouraging and helping him at each step of the process, even going as far as "changing the rules of the game" so he did not have to invest years in getting a PhD but could earn it in a single year. For David, we see only a brief mention of being helped by a well-placed person (a letter of support to avoid dismissal), as he had to struggle mightily through medical school, facing unjust hardships and discouragement along the way. Not until he entered residency in Birmingham do we read of a well-placed person—the head of the department—taking an interest in him. From that point, as we shall learn in the next chapter, Dr. David thrives, doing amazing things for God in his profession and in the community. Clearly, just as for the men Professor Royster studied, the three of us had profound differences in our experiences.

The kingdom building block here is essential. We, as Christians, have an amazing opportunity to change the structure of networks and connections (Building Block 7). God tells us our primary identity is that we are his children. Fellow Christians are, by definition, our siblings. We are to help one another. We can let the world struggle with false divisions like race. As Christians, we are empowered to overcome these divisions in our communities. God has given us the path. We shall return to this kingdom building block in the second portion of the book. But first, we turn to the final chapter of this portion of the book, considering our adult years and the lessons learned.

---

3. Royster, *Race and the Invisible Hand*, 178.

4

Grown-Up Times

In this final chapter of part 1, we discuss our lives after our formal education years were completed. We attempt to cover a great deal of time—more than thirty years at the time of this writing—by summarizing and drawing on only significant events that help point us to our final kingdom racial change building blocks. We continue to find surprises, and we continue to see God working wonders. The building blocks identified in this chapter include when God puts us in a position to help others of different racial groups thrive, we need to do so (Building Block 8), cross-racial relationships are essential for kingdom racial change, but the type of relationships and contact matters (Building Block 9), we must directly address whatever creates inequality between God's people (Building Block 10), and significant change often occurs through social movements (Building Block 11). As in the previous chapters, what these building blocks mean and why they matter will reveal themselves through our stories and analysis.

Rev. Ev.

After I left college to help my family make ends meet, we continued to struggle for several years, moving from place to place and trying to hold down jobs. There came a breaking point for my family and me. It was at that point that my best friend David, in May 1986, asked if I wanted to spend some time with him in Springfield, Illinois. David was in medical school at the time and thought his friend could use a break. So, I headed down to Springfield, Illinois, for a week.

David did not know all that was happening with my family and me, but he knew in his heart I was struggling. I had just recently gone to

Part 1. Telling the Stories amid National and Local Realities

an Air Force recruitment office, thinking that might be a good way to a steady job with money to send to my parents. But it wasn't right for me. I was feeling directionless and lost.

The intended one week with David turned into nearly a month away from Chicago. The time and distance cleared my head and gave me perspective. It set me on a course that would change my life. David asked me to go with him at the end of June to a Christian young-adult retreat. Feeling a call, I agreed to attend the retreat with David. I am thankful to God I did.

The retreat was completely life-changing for three reasons. First, my friendship with David took yet another huge step forward, especially after we survived a harrowing boating incident in which we both came close to drowning.

Second, I met a young woman, Tracie Bolton. I was smitten by her, deeply influenced by her faith, and knew we were meant to be together. A year later, we became husband and wife and have been together ever since. We have raised our four children, faced life's struggles, and been engaged in a lifetime of ministry.

Third, and connected to the first two, I felt a strong call to ministry at the retreat. I had been doing ministry since my teenage years, but at the retreat, I felt called to serve the Lord. At that point, God gave me direction. Then God opened doors despite many struggles along the way.

After the retreat, I returned to Chicago, and within a few weeks, I was interviewing for the position of youth director of Circle Urban Ministry (thanks to my then-new girlfriend, now my wife). Circle is a comprehensive, multicultural Christian organization formed to help meet the needs of poor African Americans on the west side of Chicago. It has a strong message of racial reconciliation and community empowerment, with multiple ministries under one roof.

I had experience leading youth. As noted in an earlier chapter, David and I were leading youth at our church from a young age. Though I was now just in my twenties, I had been doing youth ministry for nearly ten years. The youth director's position at Circle paid $21,000, a livable salary at that time. I was excited to interview for it with the assistant director of Circle.

But after an excruciating twelve-plus hours of interviews across three days, I was told I did not have enough experience for the job. Instead, I was offered the position of teen coordinator at a salary of $12,500.00 a year, not a livable wage. The position would have me work with youth (first boys only) from twelve to seventeen years of age.

This position was not what I interviewed for, but I was curious as to what they would say next. So I stayed to meet the executive director. The assistant director and I walked down a long hall to the executive director's office. He invited me in, but he did not stand from his chair to greet me. He only held out his right hand as he sat behind his desk with his legs crossed on top of it. I felt totally disrespected, but I decided to stay in his office at least long enough to hear what he had to say.

After twenty minutes of him lecturing me for not having enough experience, I thanked him for his time but told him I would not be taking the teen coordinator's job. As I left the building in a hurry, the assistant director tracked me down and asked me what happened.

I told him I did not take the offer as teen coordinator and that I felt mistreated. He said to me, "Don't let a white man chase you out of what's yours." I told him I felt so disrespected and just couldn't see myself working for such a person.

The assistant director then offered me two tickets to their banquet that night with special-guest speaker Rosie Grier, a famous former NFL defensive lineman. I thanked him and accepted the tickets. I invited Tracie to attend with me.

The Lord spoke to my heart during the banquet, changing my perspective. I felt the call to get the experience I needed to one day serve as the youth director. So I walked over to the table of the executive director of Circle Urban Ministries and said, "If the position of teen coordinator is still available, I will take it." He said, "Yes, it is still available, and can you start on Monday?"

I started on day one with a sum total of zero, nada, absolutely no youth. I began recruiting youth from the playgrounds as well as the middle schools, the community, and the one main high school. After eight months, I had recruited thirty to forty boys from the ages of twelve to seventeen.

About fifteen of the originally recruited young people became my leadership team. They were the ones I bounced my ideas off of, and they had plenty to add. Together we made all the rules and regulations that our new youth program would follow. The youth felt empowered as they helped me in almost every detail. Some of the rules they came up with were impossible for me to implement, such as no smoking or cursing on the block of the building. It would be the youth who would ensure rules like that would be followed.

Part 1. Telling the Stories amid National and Local Realities

All who entered our youth building had to abide by the rules and regulations set and carried out by the youth leadership team. No one dared to cause trouble in the building—or, should I say, *their* building. During the entire four years I was leading the program, we had no fights and no items stolen from our lockers, even though we did not use locks. We never had the walls or floors tagged with graffiti or gang signs. The youth declared an all-gang truce when coming on the block or being in the building. Only they could uphold those kinds of rules; it would have overwhelmed me even to try. It was amazing, to say the least.

After four years on the job, the Lord blessed us immensely, and we grew beyond what we could have ever imagined. We now had *more than seven hundred* young people enrolled in our youth program. With such numbers, we needed resources. The Lord helped me to be the most effective first-time fundraiser of all the other program directors, raising more than $37,000.00 in my first three months of going out on the fundraising circuit. The ministry was making a big difference in the lives of hundreds of young people and their families.

I did the work of the youth director and had a track record that more than proved it. But in the leadership's eyes, I was just not good enough to hold the title of youth director. After being turned down for the position again, and with a now-pregnant wife and the need for more income, I explored other options.

Circle's executive director heard through the workplace grapevine that I was unhappy with how I'd been treated during my four years with Circle. He decided to take me to lunch to have a talk with me. Circle Urban Ministries is located in the middle of Chicago's Austin community on the far west side, where about 98 percent of the residents are African Americans. But the executive director chose to take me to the whitest restaurant he could find in the mostly white suburb of Oak Park. I was the only Black man there, which I do not believe was a mere coincidence.

He started our lunch by saying: "So I heard you plan to quit if I don't raise your salary to $25,000 a year."

I responded: "When I started four years ago, I was told that I did not have the experience to be the youth director, because my most extensive work with youth was co-running the youth program in my home church. After two years as the teen coordinator and growing Circle's youth program from zero youth to more than 150, I reapplied for the youth director position. I was told I had no experience raising funds, and all the various directors of programs at Circle had to know how to raise funds. So, I trained in how to raise funds. I learned all I could and went out to all the other directors' fundraising events. After waiting a year to be green-lighted to raise funds, God allowed me to bring in three times my salary in the first three months."

"So now you feel you should get the title of youth director and make $25,000 a year?"

"It's been four years now, and yes, I do believe I've earned the position of youth director, hands down."

"So, you think you're so good now at fundraising because you had some first-time successes? You had a good start, but you're getting too big for your britches. Fundraising is fickle. Look, we changed your title to youth coordinator, and we raised your salary to $18,500, yet you seem so ungrateful."

"Circle, in my eyes, has the very best youth program in the city of Chicago. The salary you pay me now is still $2,500 less than the youth director's salary was four years ago. I was single when I first applied here four years ago. I have a family now, and my wife is pregnant with our first child. And I'm willing to take on $15,000 of the salary myself, while still working hard at fundraising to raise at least another $40,000 for Circle's youth program. I cannot afford to do what I love anymore and be a good provider to my family without higher pay.

"When I started, we had zero youth and a broken-down gym. Now we have a nice gym, thank God, and in four short years, over seven hundred youth enrolled in our program. Our boys are doing much better in school and thinking about better futures. The community respects what's happening here, and the parents have gotten behind their children. That's why we are the best in the city. The Austin community has a place that God is using to change lives for the better."

"I know a lot of good things are taking place. Let us see how the next fundraising cycle goes and revisit you being our youth director then."

"After all I just said, you sound the same as you did four years ago. What you're saying is I should just wait and see. In my mind, what you should be saying at this point is, 'Hey, man, I've seen your good works and how well the youth program has taken off under your leadership. We would be honored to offer you what you have so greatly deserved.' But instead, you are saying, 'Wait until the next fundraising time, and we'll see how you do.' Thank you for the lunch, but I cannot say this has been a good meeting."

Part 1. Telling the Stories amid National and Local Realities

With a bright red face and his fist balled up, he said: "I'm sorry you feel that way. I thought we covered some good ground."

With that, our lunch meeting ended. I had a bad taste in my mouth, and it wasn't from the food. I knew my time there was done. I had been offered a position as a church-based community organizer for the Developing Communities Project (DCP). I wasn't 100 percent sure of what that all entailed, but still, I gave my two weeks' notice in December, and sadly, my time as a youth worker was over. It was among the most difficult things I have ever done—leaving the youth. But I had to provide for my growing family.

Tracie had our first child, Michelle, in January, so I started my new job at DCP in February 1990 as a church-based community organizer. It was a difficult switch. The work was hard, and the hours were long. In fact, I was given a six-month probationary period with a clause that stated I could be fired if my trainers felt I could not make it as an organizer. Until my probation was over, I would only make $23,000 per year.

Organizers had to complete twenty-five one-on-one meetings per week with the community leadership, read an assigned book each week, and write a five-page paper on that book by the close of the day each Friday. I was responsible for recruiting at least one new pastor per month for the first six months. Finally, I had to hold what they called an "Action Meeting" at the end of the six-month probationary period. The Action Meeting—a meeting of church-based community folks to plan actions for community improvement—had to have at least 250 persons in attendance.

Setting up one-on-one meetings with leaders in the communities was hard but fun. Reading the assigned book per week and writing a five-page paper on it was tough and no fun. Yet, I must admit I learned a great deal in the process. Meeting with pastors and recruiting churches into DCP was hard but quite interesting. To have my first Action Meeting, I had to learn how to work on issues in the community, such as crime and drugs, education, economic development, youth, and housing. My Action Meeting had to be centered around issues that came directly from meeting with community leaders and the churches I would be working with, rather than just something I knew was wrong. What would my Action Meeting be about?

By the end of my six-month probation, I averaged thirty one-on-ones per week (the minimum requirement was twenty-five); I recruited four new pastors in my first six months (I was expected to recruit six), but

Grown-Up Times

I had more than twenty-five meetings with pastors in that time. My book reading and paper writing were done each week but at a B grade average. My Action Meeting was set up in the fastest-growing church on the south side of Chicago for the last Saturday in August. My main trainer recommended I not be kept on unless I took another six-month probation.

When that was brought to me, I flat-out rejected that idea. It felt too much like what I went through at Circle Urban Ministries.

I countered with my willingness to do one more month of a probationary period but with my salary raised to $27,000. With a handshake, I was told if I could do the things I said I would, they would honor the $27,000 increase. That would happen only after my first Action Meeting in August. July was the end of my first six months, but I would have to wait until the end of August to see the financial fruits of my labor.

God blessed me, and over 650 people attended my first Action Meeting! We didn't focus on one issue but four: crime and drugs, economic development, youth, and the housing problems in the community. On top of that, eight new pastors whom I recruited to the organization were in attendance. Such had never been done before in DCP's history. I was offered a permanent position and told that because of my success I would meet the founder of the organization when he returned home from Harvard Law School in about a month.

The founder was a young man with a strange name, Barack Obama. There was a buzz about this young man every place I visited in both the Roseland and Altgeld Garden communities (where David grew up). People repeatedly told me how special this Barack Obama was. For me, it got to the point where I needed to meet him just to see if his feet touched the ground when he walked.

I first met with Barack Obama in the Hyde Park community at a restaurant he frequented. The meeting was set for breakfast on Thursday at 9:30 a.m. I got to the restaurant at about 9:15 a.m., sat down, and waited for the person everyone I met said was bound for greatness. Some community leaders in Altgeld Gardens even told me that, one day, this young man would be president of the United States. Who in the world could be impressive enough to be given such high expectations? Is that even fair to throw something out like that on a person? He came into the restaurant right at 9:30 a.m. He said no words but put on a big smile and walked straight over to me. He was a tall, thin, light-skinned African American man. With an outstretched hand, he stood up and said, "Michael, right?" I said, "Right. You must be Barack." And we sat down together.

We started talking about DCP and how the greater Roseland communities were his old stomping grounds. In just those few moments, I could see he had great presence, charisma, and charm. He said he had heard a lot about the organizing I had been doing. When I described my first community Action Meeting at Salem Baptist Church, he clapped his hands and said, "Good job!"

I asked him what it was like starting a community organizing group. He told me he did not start DCP but was named its first community organizer and later given the title of executive director. Then I said to him: "Barack, I've been told that one day you are going to be president of the United States."

He paused for a second or two, then started laughing uncontrollably. When he composed himself, he stated, "With a name like Barack Hussein Obama, I would never have a chance running for such a high office as president. And I won't change my name to please people. I tried the name-change stuff before and went by Barry when I was younger. I found the best thing I can do is be myself, and people will either accept me or reject me. But, to be honest, I have been thinking about running for mayor of Chicago after I graduate from Harvard."

He then changed the subject, and we talked more about the communities I lived and worked in and how he felt Chicago was now his home no matter what else he planned to do in his life. With a shake and a hug, the meeting was over. As far as first impressions go, he was off the chart. It turns out he is not even a full year older than me.

After he graduated from Harvard Law School as the first Black editor of the *Harvard Law Review*, I had many other meetings and encounters over the years with Barack. He even sat across from me when he decided to work out of DCP's office to run his successful voter registration drive (with over one hundred thousand registrations in ten months). The staff's favorite time being around Obama was when he would, without notice, say, "I have the keys to the university's gym; who's up for a little B-ball?" We all would keep our gym shoes at the ready.

After several good years as a church-based community organizer, I became a trainer and then a lead trainer. DCP's organization had grown to twenty-seven churches, thirty block clubs, seventeen community day cares, fifty community organizations, and five community elementary schools, and we worked with more than fifteen hundred families in the Roseland, Pullman, Altgeld Gardens, and West Pullman neighborhoods. We were by far the largest community organization on the south side of Chicago.

In time, I was named the assistant director of DCP. I was in charge of the staff and most day-to-day work assignments. In 2002, I started the Urban Training Institute (UTI), which now does all the training for DCP's staff and the four leadership training retreats each year. DCP would no longer have to pay others for the training, saving about $35,000 a year.

In December 2007, I was named the executive director of DCP, the very position Barack Obama once held. We had grown significantly since the early days, and it seemed to me we needed to adapt better to that growth.

But times then got very turbulent for me. I was told by a close friend and our treasurer that although I was making good changes, I was making too many at the same time. As he noted, people don't tend to handle change well, even if it is for the better.

He was right. Things took a turn on me that admittedly caught me off guard. By late June 2008, I was fighting for my professional life at DCP. Though I was once the golden child, there were now people in DCP not even willing to look me in the eyes. I had exposed a few practices that made me the enemy of some. The board of directors would not let me take any active part in board meetings. I was told I would be made aware of what took place at the board meeting by a letter written to me by the board president within two weeks after each board meeting. It is, of course, impossible to run an organization like that, and they knew it.

I eventually had to exit the role and the organization. It was a difficult season. I had risen to be the executive director but was now unemployed.

What I did next needs explanation. I had met a pastor named Dr. Benjamin Johnson back in 1991. After our first meeting, he said to me, "Young man, I'm going to tell you something I believe you know already. God has given you the anointing as a pastor on your life. My question to you is, what do you plan to do with it?

I told him, "Yes, I have heard that before, and that's something I've never wanted to do, so I never pursued the calling. I would need God to speak to me directly. I'm sure someone else would make a far better pastor than me." I was a junior deacon, took on many other ministry roles, and sang in the choir. I was willing to do whatever was asked of

Part 1. Telling the Stories amid National and Local Realities

me except consider being the pastor of a church, no matter how many prophecies I was given that said one day I would.

Yet, for the next nine years, two to three times a month, I would meet with Dr. Ben Johnson, pastor of Christ Community Church and professor at Moody Bible Institute, to go over community issues and go through the Bible together from Genesis to Revelation and back. He had more Bible training than my father and I or even Pastor Lewis, my pastor. Our times working together were incredible.

God didn't give up on me. One day, I was walking to my car in the parking lot of a local restaurant. As clearly as a person standing next to me, for the first time I heard the voice of the Lord speak to me. God said directly to me, "I will continue to bless you, but you will never receive my greatest blessing until you do what I have called you to do for all these years."

There it was. The Lord spoke to me directly to be a pastor. This had never before happened to me. It was stunning. There was no middleman, but the message was given to me directly. It was not just an impression, but the audible voice of the Lord! No more could I say, "That's for someone else." The Lord spoke to me in a parking lot of all places. Believe me, I had to look around to see if anyone else heard what just happened to me. The voice was that clear.

So, finally, I accepted the call. I told my wife and father about my parking-lot experience. Later, I told Dr. Johnson. In the next eight months, he intensified our training and put together a special ordination board of pastors of seven different denominations. I knew I did not want to be part of a certain denomination of a church at that time, so we sought the Lord and formed a nondenominational church.

Our church's name came from the leading of the Lord through my middle daughter, Alisha. While praying and seeking the Lord, she was impressed that the church should be called New Beginnings Ministry of Faith Church. I agreed, and we all said, "Amen." That was in April 2000.

We had a special ordination service in November 2000. I would be tested by the specially selected grouping of seven pastors formed by Dr. Johnson. Those pastors officially ordained me to become the pastor of the church. Tracie, my family, and my parents became the first official members.

I would be the pastor of New Beginnings for the next seven years. In that time, we moved to twelve different places. At our sixth anniversary, I told the church of about fifty-five members that our church would have to close its doors if we didn't have a permanent home by our seventh anniversary.

Pastoral work—on top of my other full-time job, which was demanding at least seventy hours a week—was taking a massive toll on my health. My blood pressure was 215/245! Doctors told me that if I kept up my weekly schedule, I was sure to have a deadly stroke. I was already having terrible headaches and only getting, at best, two hours of sleep a night.

Before our seventh church anniversary, we did find a permanent location and we had enough money to put down on it. The problem? No one but my wife and children were willing to have church there. So, in 2007, our church doors were closed on our seventh anniversary. I gave back all the tithes and offerings we still had in the bank according to the records of how members had given.

We all cried for most of the anniversary. I felt I had let God, my family, our members, and myself down. You can imagine how bad I felt emotionally. Around the same time, I also was being pushed out of DCP, a career I'd been in for eighteen years. My frustration and hurt were off the chart. My health was hanging on by a thread on my best days.

At that time, we started attending a small church in Chicago's Roseland neighborhood called Roseland Bible Church. Tracie found the church after looking for a place where we could keep our young children involved. I went to support the family, but I was still struggling with all the turmoil I'd been through.

Yet, within a few months, I was helping around the church and taking the opportunity to share in various services, doing what I could to help the church move forward. That's when I got a call from a pastor who asked me if I could speak at one of his friends' churches in his place. I told him I would.

I ended up speaking there so often that when the eighty-four-year-old Pastor Leigh went into semi-retirement, he asked me to take his place eventually. I thought this was the special new thing God wanted me to do. I sensed this was God's will. So, after speaking with Tracie, I told Pastor Leigh and the Ingleside Community Church of the Nazarene that I would be his assistant pastor. I did that for the next two years. Then, in March 2009, I was named the new pastor of the church. My family and I served the Lord at Ingleside of the Nazarene for ten years.

Part 1. Telling the Stories amid National and Local Realities

Notice God's timing. I was in a major career transition, and that is exactly when God opened this door. Life is difficult, ministry even more so, yet God stands, providing.

Let me end my section with an important note. During this time, David McFadden and I—who had drifted apart due to our busy lives—renewed our friendship and started going on outings with the men of Bethel House of Prayer, Bethel Gospel Tabernacle, and Ingleside Community Church. In 2018, not stopping yet, we began moving to found the Chicagoland Men's Unity Group. We have been called to kingdom racial change. But more on that in the second portion of the book.

Dr. David

When I completed my fellowship in nephrology at the University of Alabama at Birmingham, I wanted to return home and practice on the south side of Chicago. My wife agreed. I also wanted to return to my home church, Bethel House of Prayer, where my best friend Michael was attending. God allowed us to do both.

Part of my ministry goal in returning to Chicago was to use my training to serve the Black indigent population on the south side of Chicago. I was fortunate enough to know a well-known Black Christian nephrologist who mainly practiced on the south side of Chicago, Dr. Paul Crawford.

He was a member of an eighteen-person nephrology group, the largest at the time in Chicago, that covered the entire Chicago area and suburbs. Dr. Crawford, whose father was a prominent pastor on the south side of Chicago, was able to get me in the group. Dr. Crawford would eventually become one of my strongest mentors. He was a mature believer, and his work ethic was beyond the pale. For example, while I started doing my rounds at the hospital early—at 7 a.m. each day—he started his rounds by 5 a.m. each day. Due to his influence I, too, began starting my rounds at 5 a.m.

His faith and dedication to Jesus rubbed off on me and made me a better servant physician for Christ. As I mentioned earlier, kidney disease affects Black Americans more than any other race. Though African Americans are just 13 percent of the US population, over 35 percent of the patients on dialysis are Black. And in my location on Chicago's south side, 99 percent of my patients were Black. Because only 5.4 percent of the physicians in America are Black, I felt it all the more important that I serve the Black community.

But things got complicated. After three and half years, I had to depart from the group because they decided to sell their dialysis facilities. After much thought, prayer, and discussion with my wife, I decided to start a solo nephrology practice. I had to leave Chicago because I had a two-year, ten-mile restrictive covenant, meaning I could not open a practice in Chicago during that time.

I decided to go to another largely Black community, Gary, Indiana (just around the bend of Lake Michigan from Chicago). I also applied to two hospitals in Joliet, Illinois (forty miles from downtown Chicago), in case it didn't work out in Gary. However, I was very confident that I would do well in Gary because of the large Black community.

My confidence was misplaced. I didn't do well at all. I received few consults and thus had few patients. I was shocked! Meanwhile, I was receiving many consults in Joliet. Therefore, to put food on my table, I left Gary and concentrated on Joliet. Later, while practicing in Joliet, I discovered that many of my patients were traveling from Morris, Illinois, to Joliet (a trip of over twenty miles each way) to receive chronic dialysis. In addition, they had no acute dialysis at the Morris hospital. I subsequently went to Morris and built an outpatient dialysis facility with my partners. We also started an acute dialysis program at the hospital. The chronic and acute dialysis program provided a much-needed medical service to the community.

God works in mysterious ways. Morris is a primarily white community. About 95 percent of my practice is now in Morris, which means 95 percent of my patients are white. This was definitely not my goal! Clearly, God's plans are not our plans.

And God did indeed have a plan. For most of our patients, we are the only Black people they know. They have accepted my wife and me as their family. We have broken down many stereotypes because of our relationships. I have been practicing in Morris for over a quarter of a century. It seems this is what God intended all along.

One of the greatest opportunities that a solo medical practice affords me is that I'm able to share my faith with my patients without any restrictions. Patients have asked me to pray for their physical healing, emotional well-being, and family problems. We have Christian literature in the waiting room, which my patients often pick up. My wife, who is my manager, has also prayed with and counseled patients over the

Part 1. Telling the Stories amid National and Local Realities

phone. She is an incredible witness. Patients often say that out of all their other doctor visits, they enjoy the visit to us the most. Truly, being a nephrologist has been the most effective and fulfilling ministry in my life. And because God has us in a white community with patients who otherwise have little exposure to people of color, God uses us to help overcome stereotypes and prejudices.

I am a successful physician. I own my practice. I make more money than I even knew existed growing up. From the outside, I have lived the American Dream, a real rags-to-riches story. Yet none of this occupational and economic success has been enough to overcome many of the negative sides of being Black in the United States. Let me offer you a few examples.

In my first practice, members of our physician group could lease just about any car we wanted at the practice's expense. I decided to lease the high-end Lexus sedan. I'm not a car person, but I went for the best because it was made available. This was both a blessing and a problem. Now that I could drive a nice car, I finally personally understood what was meant by the expression "driving while Black." I was pulled over or followed by the police many times only because I was Black driving a Lexus. As the thinking goes, no Black person could afford an upscale car, so it must be stolen. I was not speeding, I did not run stop signs, and all my car lights worked. But I was a Black man driving the Lexus, which was enough to warrant suspicion and investigation over and over.

Housing is another area where my occupation and income are not sufficient to overcome my being Black. I lived in an apartment in the Altgeld Gardens housing project until I entered medical school. My wife and I built our first house—a modest home—when I was thirty-four. At the age of forty-six, when it was clear the toll my commuting to Morris was taking, we decided to live closer to the hospital. We wanted to build a beautiful home for our family and friends to enjoy. That meant the home was expensive. The process of building it was gut-wrenching. First, it took six years—yes, six years—to build, due to delays with subcontractors and due to the bank deciding not to continue my construction loan. Though I had sufficient income, the bank continued to come up with reasons why they would not continue my construction loan.

Because my construction loan was not extended, I had to use substantial cash to continue the building. The outlay of such significant cash caused me to fall behind on my income-tax payments, which caused problems, as I will detail shortly. Every financial institution I approached repeatedly denied my application for a new construction loan. For example, at one financial institution, the loan officer—who was white—visited our home under construction and stated that he didn't have a home as expensive as the one we were building, and thus, by implication, neither should we. A Black family should not have a larger home than a white family. He denied our loan application. Similarly, another white loan officer stated to me that he had never lived in a home that cost as much as ours, and so he denied us the loan. I might have explained these occurrences as simply how the industry works. But I couldn't for this fact: my white physician colleagues were obtaining these loans without difficulties, though we had similar incomes.

After rejection upon rejection, substantial wasted time, and deep worry and stress, we eventually found a bank willing to give us a construction loan. Years had passed, and thus, as I stated, it took us a full six years to get our home completed. However, once the house was completed, I had to attempt to get an actual house loan (when you build a home, you first get a construction loan, and then a house loan is used to pay off the construction loan).

A simple mortgage loan, just like all of my white colleagues readily acquired, would have solved my housing issues. It was not nearly that simple. It was, rather, a painful, humbling process. We finally were able to get a mortgage loan. However, that bank subsequently closed. We then had to obtain another mortgage from another bank, but that bank, too, shut down. So, for a third time, we had to get a mortgage loan.

This all occurred during the banking crisis, which caused multiple banks to close. During this time, many people lost their homes, especially people of color. My initial mortgage payment was doubled by my current bank when they took over the loan. They threatened to foreclose on my home if I didn't pay the complete mortgage. Because I couldn't obtain an end loan due to the high cost of the home, the current banking crisis, and average credit, I had to file for bankruptcy to prevent foreclosure. My mortgage payment increased to three times the original amount (about $21,000 a month), which I had to pay for about seven years. I did not fight this, because I had the money and I wanted to pay off the mortgage early. However, I subsequently fell behind on two payments due to an illness that required hospitalization. I then had to agree to pay $31,000 a month to keep my home. This bank has a history of discriminatory, abusive, malicious lending to Black Americans that is well documented. I had no choice but to use this bank due to the difficulty of acquiring a mortgage. As of this writing, I am having to fight the bank to keep my home. None of this would have occurred if I were a white physician with the income I had during that time.

We are the only Black family in our nearly all-white neighborhood (another unstated reason banks hesitated to approve a loan for us). We have a walking/driving path in our neighborhood. One of our neighbors still, after several years, often doesn't acknowledge us when we wave. Undeterred, we acknowledge her to make sure she is aware that we live here and that we are not possible criminals in a neighborhood where we don't belong.

Our sons attended high school in a far more diverse school district than where we live. We wanted to make sure they were not singled out for mistreatment. But here, too, we did not always succeed. For example, during my youngest son's senior year at Homewood-Flossmoor High School, he was on the lacrosse team. They were playing a lacrosse game at Lemont High School. There was a scuffle on the field. Homewood-Flossmoor was the only team with Black players. Lemont only had white players. There was a fight, and my son Josiah tried to break up the scuffle. While he attempted to do so, suddenly, from the Lemont announcers' booth, someone said over the loudspeaker, "Lynch him," clearly directed at my son.

Minutes later, I was pulling up in the parking lot after making rounds at the hospital. My wife, visibly upset, quickly approached me with what just transpired. Without hesitation and possessing holy boldness, I headed straight to the Lemont announcers' booth. Upon entering the booth, I asked, "Who shouted, 'Lynch him'?" The people in the booth became upset at my boldness. I had to calm down because an altercation was impending. No other coach or parent responded to the "Lynch him" shout. Later, I reported this to the principal and athletic director at Homewood-Flossmoor. The person who shouted "Lynch him" was suspended from attending any more games, and Lemont was taken off Homewood-Flossmoor's schedule. I felt proud and empowered that my son could see such a display of courage from his father that he will one day need for his sons and daughters. But it is infuriating that this event occurred at all. My economic "success" could not insulate my children from the reality of race.

Our family has encountered even deeper painful experiences due to our race. They are too painful and raw to share publicly. Suffice it to say, such experiences cut deeply, and having a substantial amount of formal education, a highly respected profession, and living in a nice neighborhood are not enough to overcome our skin color. We lean on God daily for healing and hope.

Michael Emerson

Upon completing my PhD, I was offered faculty positions at several colleges and universities. As my wife and I were having and raising children, I accepted a position just thirty-five miles from where we grew up so we could have easy access to family. We settled in a little suburb of the smallish city closest to where the college was located. We didn't know it—gave it zero thought, actually—but we were living our best white lives. Our world was nearly 100 percent white. Everyone in our neighborhood, everyone in our suburb, everyone that I worked with, everyone in our church, everyone in our extended families, and everyone we encountered in our daily lives was white. It was a true whiteout. I didn't notice, and if you had pointed this out to me, I would not have cared. I would have said something like, "So? What difference does it make? I just happen to live where people are white." I also would have thought you some odd liberal or self-righteous do-gooder for even bringing up such nonsense.

Four years into this process, God decided to sear into me why it mattered. In the mid-1990s, I was invited by an elder at our church (who was my uncle-in-law) to a men's gathering called Promise Keepers, founded and led by the then–head coach of the Colorado Buffalo football team, Bill McCartney. The event was being held in the Buffalos' stadium in Boulder. It was an eight-hundred-mile drive to the event, but we were excited to be part of the more than fifty thousand attendees.

Promise Keepers called men to be better Christians, better family members, and better community members. It had seven promises it asked men to keep—such as being better husbands and fathers. The conference and subsequent ones were organized around speakers teaching biblical truths on being a faithful father, a faithful church member, and the like. One of the promises—far and away the most controversial—was racial reconciliation, calling men to overcome racial division.

I was riveted by the event, but not for the reason I thought I would be. We were given a booklet to take notes, and after each talk, we were asked

Part 1. Telling the Stories amid National and Local Realities

to write down what key point God was saying to us through the talk. No matter what was talked about, I kept writing something about race, even though six of the seven talks were not on that topic. It was like my hand was writing independently of my brain: "God grieves racial division," "You are part of the problem; be part of the solution," "God is angered by that which is not a nation," "My people suffer. It must stop." And so it went. When I went back to review what I had written throughout the conference, I was swept up in an Acts 2 experience. I often describe it as God gluing my feet to a surfboard and putting me on a wave. I was simply along for the ride as the Spirit rushed over me. I have never experienced such a thing before.

At the book tent, I purchased every book I could on race and the church. I read them nonstop, not sleeping until I completed them all. I did not feel tired. My need to learn was insatiable; a whole world was opened to me that I had never seen. After I read the last book, I went back home and took a long sleep. As I slept I had a clear vision, so clear it scared me, for the implications of the vision, I knew, would forever change our family.

When I awoke, I wrestled for a time with God. "Seriously, God, did you say this? Am I supposed to tell my pregnant wife this? How will it even be possible? Okay, I will do it. Please, please, please, don't leave me hanging."

I went to Joni and told her she might want to sit down. "I had a metamorphosizing experience at the conference, honey. I can tell you more later, but for now, let me say that I have heard a direct command from God. It will not make sense, but I am more certain this is from God than I have been sure about anything. Here is what God said: *'Your family is to live as the racial minority until I tell you otherwise.'* I don't know how this is going to happen, but I do know it will mean substantial change for us. If this is really God, we will see it unfold in God's time."

My wife, pregnant and with two toddlers in tow, living in a rich web of local familial and friendship relations, stared at me and then cried. I must admit, had she been the one to tell me such news, I would have reacted similarly.

By the next morning, she had written me a heartfelt letter saying, in essence, that perhaps I had misheard, as she had not heard any such command. Wouldn't God tell us both if it was to be such a huge life change? I had no answer. I simply said I understand but cannot walk away from this command. We agreed that if God was truly in it, God would make a way—a new job, a new city, a new church. If this was God, God would do it. We just needed to keep riding the surfboard.

God was in it. Within two weeks, a position was advertised in the Twin Cities—far and away the largest metro in the state, with Minneapolis and St. Paul being far and away the most racially diverse cities in the state. It was a faculty position at the college that my wife and her sisters had attended, and the job posting said that the ideal candidate would be able to teach in seven specific areas—all the areas I specialized in. I gulped, for I knew when I applied, I would get the position. God was working.

I did indeed get that position. Next up? Where to live. The college was in an overwhelmingly white suburb. I knew we were not to live there. We got a realtor recommended to us by several white faculty members at the college I would be joining. We told the realtor only to show us homes in racially diverse neighborhoods or, to be clearer, where we are the racial minority. This slick realtor who typically sold multimillion-dollar homes suddenly got nervous and fidgety. "Ah, well, the law says we can't take race into account. So I, ah, I can't really do that. I guess if you want to find such neighborhoods, I could show you homes there. Do keep in mind, though, that you have children soon going to school. You will want quality schools for them."

And with that, he proceeded to show us dozens of homes over the next few weeks. All of them were in white neighborhoods with "good" schools. We then reminded him that he was not showing us what we were looking for, and we reminded him that if we had to find our own neighborhoods and homes, then he was of no help to us. We ended up parting ways.

Ultimately, it was an African American colleague at my new place of employment who suggested we look in his African American neighborhood on the north side of Minneapolis. When we did find a home, it was a miracle. My wife had thrown out a fleece. This farm girl wanted to live in a farmhouse in the middle of the city. She said if that were possible, she would know God was in this. When we found the house for sale in north Minneapolis that best fit our budget and our family, we investigated it. It turns out that it was an original farmhouse that had now become part of dense blocks of homes in the city. Look at God.

God then directed us to a church. An African American pastor from Mississippi, who had been an offensive lineman for the University of Southern Mississippi football team, had recently planted a church in

Part 1. Telling the Stories amid National and Local Realities

the Twin Cities with the intent of being Black-led and racially diverse. Through connections we developed, we began attending, and it was a powerful shaper of our young family. We developed several lifelong friends there and were deeply influenced by the patient and powerful teaching of our pastor, Scottye Holloway. We were impacted by the struggles so many in the congregation faced in their daily lives and by their steadfast, dynamic faith in the face of those struggles. The level of support people gave to one another was something we had not encountered before.

I recall when our very young son debuted as a solo drummer for the Christmas pageant, having been taught by our director of worship. Just five years old, he was timid due to his age, the limited time he had played the drums, and playing in front of the congregation. Even before he began playing "The Little Drummer Boy," congregational members started shouting out their support: "You go, little Anthony," "Come on, now, God is with you," "You got this." I could see him absorb the words of encouragement. When he began, people ratcheted up the support: "Yes!" "You are doing great," "Let God flow through you, little man!" The clapping, amening, and shouts of joy for him as a member of the church body empowered our young, timid son to find joy in playing for his extended family. God can.

After a year or so into our new life, our oldest child was due to start kindergarten. Where should he attend? The African American professor who told us about his neighborhood also told us where his children attended school, an "inner-city" Catholic grade school headed by an African American principal. The school cost $1,000 a year, but that was charged only to those who could afford it. It was 90 percent African American with a small mix of other students.

The school leadership held an information session one evening for parents potentially interested in sending their children to school there. As we approached the school, the bars on the windows suggested this was a different environment than the small-town schools where my wife and I grew up. My wife was nervous about whether this was the school for our children. However, after truly connecting with the principal and learning more about the school at the information session, she agreed to get in line to put down a deposit to enroll our child, though she still felt uncomfortable about whether this was the school for our children.

As we stood in line, she left to use the restroom. Just as she disappeared, a woman came into the school screaming that the windows in her car had been busted out. For a time, it was quite a scene of mayhem. As soon as the school leaders could calm the woman down and go outside with her, my wife returned, never knowing anything had happened. I didn't tell her, and we enrolled our oldest child. He went on to attend several grades there and was joined by his brother as he turned old enough to start school. Both will tell you they have only positive and warm memories of the school, the teachers, and their classmates. God does.

And God keeps calling. After several years in Minneapolis, God called us to Houston, Texas, a difficult move for us northerners. But God communicated clearly to us. The cycle of finding a neighborhood, home, church, friends, and schools repeated, with God making it happen every step of the way. We spent fifteen years there. In our large neighborhood of several thousand people, our four children were the only white children. Interestingly, in our church and their schools, this wasn't always the case, but it became more so over time due to "white flight" and, in our view, some questionable rezoning practices.

We learned so much during this time, but we put our Houston house up for sale when God called us to move again. We had built our house for $273,000 and put a substantial amount into it over the years we lived there. When it came time to sell, to our shock, the appraisal said our house was worth only $160,000, which was all we could sell it for. This was a substantial financial loss that had painful economic impacts for many years. Still, my family and I continued to be punished. It turns out that when you "short sell" your home, you can't get a conventional mortgage loan for the next four years. If you need a larger loan in an expensive market, you are required to wait seven years. Such was the case for us. So, forced to make a short sale by government regulations and appraisal practices, we were punished for the next seven years for something completely out of our control.

After fifteen years in Houston, we were called to Chicago. Again, the cycle repeated itself. By this time, only our youngest daughter was still in high school, and God provided her with a deeply enriching school and a set of racially diverse friends. We ended up living in an overwhelming Hispanic neighborhood and later in a strongly African American area of Chicago, just outside downtown. During our time in Chicago, I had the privilege of encountering Rev. Ev. and Dr. David. They invited me to speak at their Unity Group. Because it was during COVID-19's early days, the talk and my first meetings with them were online. Eventually, over a few years, we met in person, shared meals, had our wives meet, discussed Dr. David and Rev. Ev's vision, talked about how God desires for all his people to thrive, and eventually germinated this book.

Conclusion

We have not attempted an exhaustive narrative of our post-formal-education adult years but have highlighted some significant events along the way. We can learn much by looking comparatively at our adult lives.

All of us exist in leadership structures. Either we are a leader, or we are under a leader, and quite often, it is both. The goal of leadership is to enable people to live into the gifts, talents, and abilities God has given them for the betterment of the whole (be that whole an organization or a society). To do so, a leader must *inspire* people toward a vision, *empower* people through resources, structure, and instilling confidence, and *unleash* people to thrive on behalf of the whole. A leader must, therefore, be willing to make difficult decisions that further the vision and mission of the organization.

The great tragedy of so much leadership is that it stifles people, deeply injuring society overall, robbing us all of the contributions that could be made. Too often in too many organizations, leaders see their role as command and control, as needing to fit people into roles the leadership has predetermined. Too often, we limit what people can do by having too small of expectations, being too distrustful of others, micromanaging, wanting full control, worrying that others might outshine us, or simply not caring enough to want to empower people. All such behaviors are not only the antithesis of leadership, but they are also inefficient, harmful to organizations, and a damaging downward pull on society. They deny us all of the flourishing God intended for the beloved community.

It should be obvious that this type of control is poor leadership. But we see it in organization after organization. Certainly, we saw evidence of this across our stories. For Rev. Ev., despite his clear gifting in the youth ministry he led under the umbrella of a larger Christian ministry, he was not promoted and ultimately not encouraged to flourish. He was constantly told to wait, to get more training, to get more experience, and to raise more money. No matter what he did, he was asked to do more.

He was, in essence, being told he was never enough. And this was just to be promoted to youth director, not the head of the organization.

The sad reality is that this treatment drove him away from a thriving ministry, leaving hundreds of young people without their mentor and spiritual leader. The race component (Rev. Ev. being Black, his boss white) made this instance all the more devastating. As Christians, we must see God in each person, doing what we can to help them thrive. So, we plead: Leaders, no matter your management level over others, be great at your job! Care about others, care about your organization, care about humanity. Show that you care by learning how to lead. Made in the image of the Almighty, all humans have gifts. Leaders find those gifts—at the time of hire, while employed, while volunteering—encourage them, develop them, and direct them for the good of the whole. If we are not doing that, we should not be in leadership.

As we consider how to move toward kingdom racial change, we are pointed, then, to a building block: when God puts you in a position to help others of different racial groups thrive, do so (Building Block 8). Let us not stifle God's creation. Inspire, empower, unleash, and the blessings will flow.

In this book, we have talked much about social structures—the way we organize ourselves as groups of people and as societies. We have done so with good reason, as the existing social structures create an unfair playing field designed to benefit some over others. But within social structures, we can never overemphasize the importance of relationships. We see evidence of this importance across all of our life stories—Rev. Ev. learning about openings from his girlfriend (now wife), Dr. David getting his first position through connections within his community, Emerson being influenced by several personal connections, and all of us being discipled in our faith by caring mentors. For many years, a dominant perspective of American Christianity has been that racial division can be overcome by developing relationships across racial groups. Doing so is indeed a positive and necessary development. It is not sufficient, but it is necessary.

We have a social-science theory and a long set of research studies around developing personal relationships and racial change. It is called contact theory and is, at its root, quite simple: those who have contacts across race will have less racial prejudice and engage in less racial discrimination. This is because they will come to understand not just categories but actual people and their actual experiences. They will develop empathy for racial others, and eventually the racial others will no longer be "others."

Thousands of studies have been undertaken to test this seemingly simple thesis. It turns out the process is more complicated than we might expect. For example, research has had to spend a great deal of time determining what type of contact matters—is it merely being exposed to diverse others, such as in a diverse high school, or is it having acquaintances such as those you work or worship with, or is it having close friendships?

Interestingly, "contact" can have the exact opposite effect than the theory predicts, where people become more prejudiced as diversity increases. This often occurs when a community becomes more diverse, as people can feel threatened by the diversity, believing their livelihood or way of life is under threat. But in most cases, interracial contact has the expected positive effects, especially if there is long-term contact and friendships. A diverse school or church setting can help substantially by being a recurring gathering point for friendships to form and cooperation to occur.

The word *cooperation* matters. If people of diverse racial perspectives are put together in situations where their cooperation benefits them all, the impact of those cross-racial contacts is substantial and positive. Of course, the converse is true as well: if people are put in competitive situations, racial contact heightens racial division.

We want to draw attention to the initial offering of the theory in 1954 by a professor named Gordon Allport. He suggested that the positive effects of intergroup contact will occur when four conditions are met: (1) intergroup cooperation (as noted above), (2) equal status of those in contact, (3) common goals, and (4) support by authorities.[1]

More than seventy years of research has overwhelmingly supported the necessity of these four conditions. People must meet in arenas where they are not competing against each other, where instead they cooperate to meet a common goal, where they have the full blessing and support of those in charge (for example, a pastor encouraging the congregational members to serve together across race in ministries of the church or community), and, in the most difficult condition to meet, where they are of equal status.

Why is the equal-status condition the most difficult to meet? Because our society's entire history has been about creating racial inequality.

---

1. Gordon Allport, *The Nature of Prejudice* (Boston: Addison-Wesley, 1954).

Grown-Up Times

A quick look at current data shows just how effective our society has been in creating racial inequality. White people have, on average, ten times or more the wealth of Black, Hispanic, and Native American people. White people have longer life expectancies, get sick less, get paid more for similar jobs, on average have higher-ranked jobs, are exposed to less crime, pay lower interest rates on loans, go to prison less for the same crimes as others, pay less taxes when they have comparable income as others, have more access to quality education, and are given by default more status than are other groups. We often summarize this reality in this way: white people are assumed to be middle-class (or higher) unless they can prove otherwise; Black, Hispanic, and Native Americans are assumed to be lower-class unless they can prove otherwise.

And prove it they attempt to do. Those in groups assumed to be lower-class engage in what is known as conspicuous consumption. That is, to demonstrate they are not lower-class, they spend greater percentages of their income on markers of "success" in our society, things like cars, homes (when possible), and clothes. Since we rarely know what people make, we signal our financial success with stuff. This then means those assumed to be lower-class must spend more of their resources on signaling success.

Dr. David discussed how God led him to serve an overwhelmingly white clientele in his medical practice. He and his wife have contact with racial others, and he notes how he often is among the very few people of color his patients encounter. He also talks about the ministry afforded him in this situation—his patients admire and appreciate him and his family, leading to openings for ministry and sharing the gospel. God knows contact theory! See, in this case, how God made possible the single most difficult condition of contact theory to be met: white people are coming to a trained Black man for his knowledge and ability to help them. In this context, his status is not assumed to be lower-class. He is an equal. As such, the contact can and does have a positive effect.

It doesn't work this way in all situations for Dr. David, as he details for us. Even making the salary he does and living in the neighborhood he does, many people along the way continue to view him as lower-class, because they do not truly know him. They only see him as Black and thus assign the many stereotypes and expectations they have for such a category.

We have a building block here, and it is this: cross-racial relationships are essential for kingdom racial change, but the type of relation-

Part 1. Telling the Stories amid National and Local Realities

ships and contact matters (Building Block 9). We must strive for cooperation and shared goals, have the full support of authorities, and meet as equals. This latter requirement, so difficult in our society, is solved by our Lord. As Christians, we are commanded to drop any worldly definitions of status and draw on our true advantage—we are equal in Christ, each created for service to God. No one is better; no one is worse in God's family. Under these conditions, we must strive to build a dense web of cross-racial relationships and social situations that help us do so, such as racially diverse churches and cross-racial ministries.

We have another massive lesson from this chapter, one that is difficult for us on our own to notice but impacts millions of us every day. The main way that most Americans build wealth in the United States is through home ownership. Whatever else the American Dream is, it always includes owning a home that increases in value over time. It is a simple truism—buy a home, and its worth appreciates, generating access to wealth to be used to buy an even nicer home, to gain funding for other endeavors, or to serve as a retirement nest egg.

But it doesn't work this way. It is a lie. And it is a lie because this promise only works for some by making it not work for others. Let us explain by first focusing on Emerson's experience. He and his family built a new home in a newly developing community and subsequently invested a substantial amount in landscaping, curtains, upgraded features, and the like. His neighborhood was 80 percent African American, 16 percent Hispanic, and 4 percent other. When Emerson needed to sell the home seven years later because he and his family were moving to a new city, the appraisal said the home had not appreciated at all. In fact, the appraisal concluded that the home had *declined* in value by 41 percent. How could this be? The home was beautiful, extremely well cared for, and upgraded since it was first built.

Emerson suspected it was because he lived in a minority neighborhood, and given our lesson above, that minorities are (wrongly) considered lower-class by default, so are their neighborhoods. Thus, in an overwhelmingly minority neighborhood, Emerson's individual characteristics—white, doctorate, working for a prestigious university, with a well-cared-for home—simply didn't matter as much as the neighborhood characteristics. Appraisals are based on the value of recently sold homes in the same general area, not on the independent assessment of a home's worth. In short, a home is only worth what other homes in the area are worth, defined by what homes sold for in the past few months, which, of course, are themselves dependent on what homes before them sold for in the previous few months before that. The American idea of rugged individualism and pulling oneself up by the bootstraps doesn't apply to home values.

Because of how the loan industry works, you can only sell your home for the appraised amount. Unless a buyer has substantial cash and is willing to pay more for a home than its appraised value (this rarely happens), the appraisal sets what your home will sell for. As such, Emerson had to take a 41 percent loss on his home.

When Emerson shared this unfortunate reality with town officials, with local business owners, and with city boosters, the response was telling. Emerson was blamed. No, the system is not unfair, he was told. He should have gotten another appraisal. He should not have lived in that community. He sold at the wrong time. He should have waited for values to increase. He should have rented the home (Emerson checked into this—he could not have rented it for an amount high enough to cover the mortgage). He probably overpaid for the home when he purchased it, and the market was simply correcting itself. He should have researched the worth more before he purchased the home.

How interesting. In a system that has little to do with individuals, it was the individual being blamed for this "failure of the American Dream." Emerson became curious. Was there something behind his thought that some communities' home values are deflated and others are inflated merely because of the race of those who live there? He suggested this idea to two of his graduate students, and they undertook several years of research to answer the question. The findings are stunning.

First, we found a study published in 2003 that focused on Milwaukee, Wisconsin.[2] The author asked, If in 1970 you purchased a home in Milwaukee for $40,000, what was it worth in 1993? Through painstaking data collection and analysis, he found that for white residents, their homes had appreciated on average to $250,000, an amazing increase of $210,000, or in percentage terms, an increase of more than 600 percent. The American Dream lives!

But for Black residents (Milwaukee during this time was overwhelmingly Black or white), their 1970 $40,000 homes were worth in 1993, on average, just $32,000, a 20 percent value *decrease*. That was the first

2. Kim Sunwoog, "Long-Term Appreciation of Owner-Occupied Single-Family House Prices in Milwaukee Neighborhoods," *Urban Geography* 24, no. 3 (2003): 212–31.

Part 1. Telling the Stories amid National and Local Realities

evidence that Emerson's experience was not an isolated one, but it wasn't good enough. It was based on data from several decades before the current times, and it was not entirely clear that race itself led to this decline in value. It could be smaller homes, less well-cared-for homes, or other factors.

So, his graduate students did the same study in Houston, updating it by using the 2005–2015 period and holding constant factors like neighborhood poverty rates, school quality, and commuting times to work.[3] Thus, they isolated the racial composition of the neighborhood. They compared neighborhoods that were 85 percent or more white, Black, or Hispanic. What did they find? Homes in white neighborhoods of Houston appreciated over this decade by an average of $82,100. The American Dream works.

But not for everyone. Homes in Hispanic neighborhoods declined in value by an average of $4,400. Homes in Black neighborhoods declined even more, by an average of $26,500. The American Dream is a failure. Emerson's experience—while living in a largely Black neighborhood during this same period—was not an isolated case. It was a feature of the entire housing market of the Houston region. Those living in white neighborhoods were being rewarded, while those living in other neighborhoods were being robbed of their investments.

But his graduate students did not stop there. As they moved to professor and research roles, they worked to access national data on appraisals and home values. Their findings are even more stunning than what they found in Houston. Growing ever more sophisticated in their analysis, they could compare average appraised values for comparable homes (same square footage, same number of bedrooms, etc.) in comparable neighborhoods (same average income, etc.) in all US metros with at least five hundred thousand people. They compared changes in appraised home values in white neighborhoods and neighborhoods of color from 1980 to 2015. They found the American Dream to be alive in white neighborhoods across the nation. On average, over this period, homes in white neighborhoods increased in value from roughly $150,000 in 1980 to nearly $400,000 in 2015.[4] Welcome to a quarter of a million in new wealth!

---

3. Junia Howell and Elizabeth Korver-Glenn, "Neighborhood Racial Biases in 21st Century Housing Appraisals," Kinder Institute for Urban Research, Rice University, Working Paper, November 11, 2015.

4. Junia Howell and Elizabeth Korver-Glenn, "The Increasing Effect of Neighbor-

But for communities of color, their home values remained essentially unchanged. No new wealth. Where is the American Dream? What is more, they found that the gap in home values between white neighborhoods and neighborhoods of color is accelerating, getting larger in absolute and percentage terms with each passing year. As a result, overall racial inequality has not declined over time. Despite whatever advances along racial lines have been made over the past several decades, racial inequality not only remains firmly entrenched but is growing.

When we take this knowledge and then read, for example, Dr. David's story of attempting to build a home and being repeatedly turned down for loans despite his substantial income, we see the process operating in real time. One of Emerson's graduate students, Elizabeth Korver-Glenn, immersed herself in the home-buying, home-selling, appraisal, and loan process to understand how it works. She found substantial racial inequality and unfairness at every single step of the process, such that it compounds to create the massive differences in wealth generation that ultimately are occurring in the United States.[5]

We desperately need a building block here, as we will never have kingdom racial change with such gross inequalities multiplying daily. We must directly address whatever creates inequality between God's people (Building Block 10). We must do so until the inequality creators are no more.

How we do this will be detailed in the book's second section. But we must end this chapter with a final lesson and building block. When Rev. Ev. worked in community organizing, we saw a vital process of how change occurs. It requires people to work together, and there is a set of best practices for working together to coordinate action for change. Thus, our final building block is that significant change often occurs through social movements, which occur through community organization and group cooperation (Building Block 11).

If you are reading this book, you likely want to know how to go about change. Armed with our building blocks, we are at last ready to turn to exactly that.

---

hood Racial Housing Composition on Housing Values," *Social Problems* 68, no. 4 (2020): 1051–71.

5. Elizabeth Korver-Glenn, *Race Brokers: Housing Markets and Segregation in 21st Century Urban America* (New York: Oxford University Press, 2021).

Interlude

We now enter the heart of the book: kingdom racial change. Recall that we defined kingdom racial change in the prelude as the desperate need for a realignment to be right again with God's intentions for his people. Kingdom racial change is the sum total of the processes that must occur for us to get back into biblical, godly alignment across racial groups. It is overcoming racial inequality, injustice, division, and indifference. It is arriving at justice, righteousness, reconciliation, unity, and community.

But this definition begs the question: Do we want to see change?

Many do not. A large group of Christians, comfortable with life or busy trying to "make it," give little thought to racial realities. Or they view such focus as patently unchristian. We are to save souls, study the Bible, and support our church family. Most anything else, for such folks, seems worldly and an unwise investment of our limited time.

Others want to see kingdom racial change but don't want to get particularly involved, don't have the time for it, or struggle with whether such a direct focus is a Christian thing.

Still others truly want to see change and want to be a part of contributing to that change. Such folks, likely the minority of Christians (though, we think, that number is growing), view the Bible and God as desiring human flourishing for everyone and nurturing for the entire church body. They will invest time and resources to move the needle for kingdom racial change. They believe, in fact, they are called to do so.

The rest of the book is for this latter group. All, of course, are welcome to read on, but our focus will now be on the change agents, those desiring to see God's work in the world being done, making right individuals, relationships, and systems.

Interlude

The founder of the Asian American Christian Collaborative, Ray Chang, says that "God is radically inclusive, inviting us all to come just as we are. But then God is radically intrusive, asking us to change."[1] We must be transformed as people and as a community to conform ourselves and our society to God's design. We are change agents. It is our Christian DNA. Anything short of this is to deny our essence and purpose. This is why working for kingdom racial change, despite the hefty challenges, is so exhilarating. Living into our purpose is where true contentment and satisfaction lie.

We already have some amazing Christian books on how to work against racism, for racial justice, for racial reconciliation, and for racial unity. Think of this book as a sociological complement to those books. You will want to read them as well. What we offer here draws upon sociological understanding in light of biblical truths to help us know *what* needs changing and to give us the wisdom for *how* to make change.

We organize this second portion of the book into three chapters based on the levels of human social existence, as we noted in the prelude. These three levels are the micro (individuals, relationships, families), the meso (social networks, organizations such as churches, and social movements), and the macro (systems, laws, policies, and entire institutions such as education). We shall approach the *what* and *how* of change by going from the macro to the meso to the micro. This order, we believe, is the proper path. We must understand the macro-level changes needed (think of this as society needing to be born again) before we can determine how to proceed for kingdom racial change. To proceed, we will then need to understand the meso-level levers that we have to help us make macro-level changes. And for that to occur, we must then consider the micro-level worlds that we all inhabit.

---

1. Ray Chang, personal interview, November 2023.

PART 2

Making Kingdom Racial Change

5

Make No Small Plans—Macro-Level Change

How exciting. Here we are, ready to detail kingdom racial change. From the first part of the book, we had three building blocks pertaining to the macro level:

1. The mighty arm of racial power is that it is systemic (Building Block 1). When Jesus calls his followers to take worldly systems and turn them on their heads, he would undoubtedly include the system of racial injustice, as it is daily gouging his people. Christians do not accept ungodly systems—including segregation—as simply the way things are. They change them.
2. Find a way to overcome the link between race and class (Building Block 6). It is an unbiblical relationship.
3. We must directly address whatever creates inequality between God's people (Building Block 10). We must do so until the inequality creators are no more.

The Bible—God's Word to us—directs us what to do. Consider the following.

> Look! The wages you failed to pay the workers who mowed your fields are crying out against you. The cries of the harvesters have reached the ears of the Lord Almighty. You have lived on earth in luxury and self-indulgence. You have fattened yourselves in the day of slaughter.
> James 5:4–5[1]

---

1. Here and throughout, unless otherwise noted, Scripture quotations are from the NIV.

Part 2. Making Kingdom Racial Change

These are direct words from the apostle James. They are meant to be direct, so the meaning is unmistakable. Unjust inequality is horrific and will end badly for those who have benefited from unjust systems. Notice the emotion James puts into these verses—an exclamation point snaps us to attention, and strong language is used: "failed to pay," "crying out," "self-indulgence," "fattened" for the "slaughter." In the first three verses of this chapter, James goes further, telling rich people to weep and wail, that their wealth is corroded, and that this very corrosion will eat their flesh like fire. The images are powerful, painful, and unambiguous.

Christians cannot tolerate such systems. They must oppose them, turning the world's ways on its head, as Jesus taught us. But what are those systems, and how would we ever be able to change them? In a world given to Satan, would we simply be wasting our time?

It turns out that systems can be changed. Humans created them, and so humans can uncreate them. Changing evil systems is a massive part of our calling as God's people. In this chapter, we shall consider some of the key systems that need changing, and we shall discuss how to change them.

Housing

Every single one of us resides somewhere. Even the homeless we have known attempt to keep a tent under the same underpass or in the same abandoned lot year after year. Housing and residence are fundamental to all humans of all times, whether nomadic peoples or people tied to particular lands, cities, or neighborhoods. In a society like the United States, housing is fundamental to our security and our dreams. This is why so many of us find homelessness disturbing. It is difficult to fathom someone living without a stable, comfortable residence.

Housing in the United States is deeply flawed, with a strong, seemingly intractable link between race, class, and neighborhood. Every city in the United States with even a modicum of racial diversity will have racially coded neighborhoods: white neighborhoods, Black neighborhoods, Asian neighborhoods, Hispanic neighborhoods, Native neighborhoods, immigrant neighborhoods, and so on.

We have earlier noted the person-on-the-street explanation for this massive pattern of racial segregation. "People prefer to live with people like themselves." We have noted why such an explanation is highly insufficient: Why is the idea of "people like themselves" based on race rather than things like family size or religion? Why would a white Christian prefer to live with secular white people over Christians of color? No white Christian would say they prefer this, yet based on where they actually live, the evidence overwhelmingly points to this conclusion.

The reason is that this fundamental human reality—housing—is color-coded in the United States. We are not racially segregated by chance. It is a system enacted by policies, laws, mores, and the day-to-day actions of millions of people. The result is an amazingly powerful and beneficial system for American whites. As we discussed in the previous chapter, American white people collectively gain immense wealth from the system, even as people of color do not. They gain access to the "best" schools, the best parks, the most services, clean streets, low crime, avoidance of exposure to high poverty, and so many other benefits.

Dr. Elizabeth Korver-Glenn and Dr. Junia Howell wanted to understand how racial segregation continues to happen and the impacts it has, especially on wealth creation. Dr. Korver-Glenn undertook an in-depth, on-the-ground study of the entire housing-market process by studying the actors at each stage. This study ranged from how developers determine where and what type of housing to develop to the impactful role of real-estate agents, to how mortgage bankers go about their business, to how appraisers determine home values. She found that at *every single step* across the entire process, race impacts decisions and actions, all to create and protect racial segregation. Check out her book *Race Brokers* to get a full understanding. In short, her research found that race-coding occurs both overtly—with outright prejudice and discrimination—and covertly—such as by using code words like "inner city" or "diverse school" to subtly steer white clients from mixed to white neighborhoods. As she concludes, "The U. S. housing market is a fundamentally racialized market that White professionals and White-dominated professional organizations maintain and animate, day after day." With the end result, she writes, "racial segregation is a process that White people actively maintain in order to maintain their power."[2]

---

2. Elizabeth Korver-Glenn, *Race Brokers: Housing Markets and Segregation in 21st Century Urban America* (New York: Oxford University Press, 2021), 171–72.

Part 2. Making Kingdom Racial Change

Who loses from this system? Although some white people lose in this system—and conversely, some people of color win—as groups, the system is set up for people of color to lose, and as research shows over and over with ever-increasing details of why, the system works dramatically well. The end result, as we have said, is massive wealth accumulation for white people as a whole, some for Asian people, and significant stunting of wealth accumulation for everyone else. And it is not just wealth that is impacted. Because school funding is tied to local property values, education is deeply impacted by the racially biased housing system. We will explore the racial inequalities in education in the next section.

This is a book about making kingdom racial change. As Christians, we want to see God's kingdom shine and the darkness recede. But how? We are not going to talk in generalities. We are going to offer real solutions and invite you to join.

Deeply motivated by her Christian faith and study of biblical texts, Dr. Junia Howell sought practical ways to overcome the severe racial injustice in housing. After extensive research into the unequal housing system and the radically different outcomes the system produces by race, after finding that the system is increasingly causing ever greater inequality, and after testifying to such inequality in front of federal congressional committees, she felt directly called to use her knowledge and skills to alter the housing system.

She began by noting that no other area is as important to Americans and the economy as housing. People spend, on average, 34 percent of their income on housing, and working-class people spend nearly two-thirds of their take-home pay on housing. What is more, a full one-third of the entire gross domestic product (GDP) of the United States is based on housing. Drawing on her sociological and economic knowledge of the housing industry through her years of careful study, Dr. Howell founded an organization called Eruka to fundamentally change the housing industry. *Eruka* means restoring equity. It combines the Latin *equitas*, meaning equity or justice, with the Hebrew word *arukah*, meaning restoration or complete healing.

Eruka's vision is a just economy, and its mission is "to cultivate equity across people and places by reimagining housing and financial services."[3] But how?

---

3. See the Eruka website, www.eruka.org, for details.

Dr. Howell's organization Eruka has four main components, and they are quite different than how we have been taught to think about housing in the past. First, she began by treating housing not just as an asset—a commodity to buy speculatively, borrow on, and sell in a shell game where some win and many lose—but as a necessity. Every human needs shelter. So, Dr. Howell sought to design a system that made that understanding fundamental to its design. The first component is what is called Eppraiser, or equitable appraisals. According to one of her videos, Eppraiser

> is a tablet and mobile application that uses public records as well as full scans of properties to identify property components. These components include all the interior finishes, as well as major systems like plumbing and electric. It also includes examinations of the exterior features like roofs, framing, and foundations. For each component we identify the cost of the original installation, its expected life span, and then we use this information to estimate the remaining use value of the component. With the remaining use value of each component we sum these together to create a total appraised value for the property.[4]

Consider how fundamentally revolutionary—and smart—this idea is: rather than housing values being based in good part on the value of other homes in your neighborhood, which is shaped by race and many other nonhousing factors, let's value homes for what the homes themselves are actually worth, as in how much they cost to build, the value of the housing components, and their remaining life span.

Would such an approach reduce the vast racial inequalities in housing values? According to Dr. Howell's calculations, simply instituting this change would result in reducing "the racial inequality in appraised values by nearly 7000%." That is correct, 7,000 percent. What a vast kingdom racial change from changing but one macro component of the American system. And the impact goes further, as such a change would create housing stock that far more people could afford, leading to more people having economically sustainable shelter.

The second component of Eruka is mortgage lending. If you have bought a home, you have a decent sense of how the system currently

---

4. Text transcribed from video "Eruka: Building a Just Economy," YouTube, 2024, https://tinyurl.com/mvkz4bnp.

works. You apply for a loan. The mortgage lender considers your credit score and other factors in deciding if they will give you a loan and, if so, the interest rate you will be charged. Let's say that interest rate is 7 percent. If you look at the "fine print," you will find that throughout the typical thirty-year loan, you will pay more than *double* what you borrowed as the interest accumulates over time. It is a severe price to pay to purchase a home, yet you are stuck with the system unless you have the cash to purchase your home without a loan. This system tells you what your interest rate will be and requires you to still have substantial cash up front for closing costs, down payments, and other assorted fees.

Eruka says no to all of that. Instead, a borrower pays in interest 10 percent of the amount borrowed, with no down payment required. So, if a home costs $200,000, in the Eruka system, you can borrow the entire $200,000 and will pay back $220,000—that is, the amount borrowed plus 10 percent. That 10 percent pays for the employees, provides additional capital for more loans, and covers the assorted government-required fees.

Consider the financial impact of this alternative loan system. At the time of this writing, the average American homeowner pays $2,991 a month for their mortgage payment. The average renter pays $1,900 a month. But with the Eruka system, the average American homeowner would pay $1,488 a month, and the average renter would pay just $915 a month. The Eruka system thus cuts the average monthly payment *by more than half*! Imagine the possibilities of opening housing to so many more people, creating greater equity in housing, and giving people more disposable money for saving, investing, starting a business, or more.

But doesn't people's ability to repay the loans need to be assessed? After all, if they receive a loan but cannot pay it back, the system quickly falls apart. Eruka does assess borrowers' ability to repay loans, but not through the opaque, complicated system of credit scores. Instead, Eruka uses a liquidity-based risk-assessment approach. It is straightforward—given your income and liquid assets, can you repay the loan? If so, you qualify.

The overall system of loans is funded through ebonds. This is the third component of the Eruka system. Individuals, churches, and other organizations can purchase Eruka ebonds. The money is used to fund home loans. As the loans are repaid, those who purchased ebonds receive their initial investment back plus 4 percent.

Finally, the last service of Eruka is essessments. This is Eruka's equitable, sustainable, and predictable approach to property taxes. As Dr. Howell explains in her video,

> This approach takes into account all the municipal resources that a local government is funding for their residents. It looks at the total cost of those and then estimates tax shares—in other words, what proportion should each parcel pay of that total amount. Those proportions are derived by looking at the infrastructural, environmental, and social costs of each parcel.[5]

In sum, the four components of Eruka will lead to substantial kingdom racial change, altering a system that is flawed, unequal, unjust, and—even to those it is designed to reward—costly. We make, then, the following straightforward recommendation: as individuals, as small groups, as congregations, and as communities, participate in the Eruka system. Buy ebonds, purchase homes, get loans. In so doing, you are benefitting both others and yourselves. It is God's math, where it is not a zero-sum game, but where everyone can gain and, in so doing, bring about racial justice.

Education

In modern society, we spend nearly all of our growing-up years in formal education. Being an informed citizen, communicating well with others, and making a sufficient living are closely tied to adequate education. The number of years of education needed keeps increasing. A grade school education was at one time sufficient, then a junior-high level of education. Soon, though, it became clear that a high school diploma was needed.

Today, increasingly, a college degree is needed, and for many professions, a master's degree is a tremendous help. But as we saw in our own stories, educational access, affordability, and support vary tremendously by race and class. Indeed, research by educational scholars finds that the performance of students is strongly connected to the average

---

5. Text transcribed from video "Eruka: Building a Just Economy," YouTube, 2024, https://tinyurl.com/mvkz4bnp.

socioeconomic status (education and income) of the parents within the school district they attend.[6] The higher the average socioeconomic status (SES) of the school district, the higher the average performance of the students in that school district, measured not only by standardized test scores but by grades ahead or grades behind where students are expected to be according to their age. Higher SES school districts have students performing up to three grades ahead of where they are expected to be, while in the lowest SES school districts, students are often performing up to three grades below where they are expected to be.

Why this relationship? At least two reasons must be mentioned. We fund school districts in good part through local taxes. The more money available in the district, the more money is generated through taxes. And though it is not the only thing that matters, the more resources available to a school—quality facilities, quality teachers, books, technology, extracurricular activities, tutoring services, and the like—the better the results for student performance. The second reason that bears mentioning is that the more resources parents have, the more they can afford supplementary education, such as private tutors, SAT/ACT training, summer camps, educational experiences, and much more.

So, we have an educational inequity problem based on socioeconomic status. But it gets worse. Because we have huge inequalities in SES by racial group, we end up finding this: the highest-performing school districts are filled with white and Asian students; the lowest-performing school districts are overwhelmingly a majority of African American, Hispanic, and Native American students.

The end result is that we have set in motion a perpetual racially unequal society in which our educational system does much of the work of racial segregation, even though it is filled with hardworking students, teachers, and administrators all attempting to overcome such inequalities.

So how do we work for kingdom racial change in education? Let's be clear that, just as in housing, change is absolutely vital. It can have a major impact since effective change can interrupt racial and economic injustice at the starting point of the next generation's educational journeys.

---

6. See, for example, Sean F. Reardon, Demetra Kalogrides, and Kenneth Shores, "The Geography of Racial/Ethnic Test Score Gaps," *American Journal of Sociology* 124, no. 4 (2019): 1164–221.

Make No Small Plans—Macro-Level Change

We can make changes at three major points in the educational journey. If you, your small group, or your church wants to contribute to educational change, choose one of these three areas.

The first area is prekindergarten. Not so long ago, there was no kindergarten. People started education in the first grade. The authors of this book all went to half-day kindergarten. It wasn't until quite recently that full-day kindergarten became the norm. Even as we write, not all states yet require full-day kindergarten.

Why the move to early and more education? Because research continually finds that starting early helps close the educational gaps that develop at home. By the time children begin formal schooling at age five, there are already massive gaps in the number of words they know, speaking ability, experience with simple math, and other differences. What happens at home matters, and as we would expect, parents of higher socioeconomic status tend to place more emphasis on education, use more advanced words and sentences with their children, and can afford to provide prekindergarten educational experiences.

A raft of research has now found that given the realities of our current society, prekindergarten formal education (for example, preschool) can have significant benefits for later educational success and can reduce racial and economic educational disparities. In some places around the nation and world, movements exist advocating for universal prekindergarten education. How this looks can vary—it could be in person, online, in home, or in another format—but the key is providing structured exposure to educational opportunities before kindergarten starts. Consider finding such an advocacy organization and supporting its work.

Second, once children begin kindergarten through high school, much can be done to work for kingdom racial change. Often, our first thought is to volunteer as tutors in an afterschool program at a local school. Such work is important but will not lead to macro educational change. Consider the complexities of students' academic performance. As teachers soon come to recognize, what occurs in students' homes and their neighborhoods greatly impacts students' ability to concentrate, learn, and perform well on exams. Consider the following areas, which are all studied by the Houston Educational Research Consortium (HERC) at the Kinder Institute at Rice University.[7]

---

7. See these details from the Kinder Institute webpage of HERC at https://tinyurl.com/yc32y543.

Student Mobility: Millions of students switch schools every year. The result? In the short term, they perform worse on standardized tests and have more social difficulties, and in the long term, they have an increased risk of dropping out, not graduating high school on time, and not attending college.

English as a Second Language: The number of students who arrive in US and Canadian schools not fluent in English is increasing substantially. Effectively teaching English to such students is imperative for subsequent academic success. Having trained, prepared instructors and a curriculum is imperative.

Funding Equity: The current system of funding our local schools is based in good part on local taxes. As we noted above, such a system results in funding inequity. Since education is a state and national concern, funding should move to such levels, greatly flattening the current extensive inequalities in educational funding.

Wraparound Needs: Students face a variety of nonacademic challenges across areas like physical health, mental health, basic needs (for example, food, housing), home learning environment, and enrichment activities. Based on extensive research, HERC recommends the following:[8]

1. Improve access to mental-health support by addressing the costs as well as the social stigma/apprehension toward seeking help.
2. Support the physical health of students and families by ensuring everyone has the opportunity and resources to attend annual checkups (doctor, dentist, and vision).
3. Prioritize connecting families with free or low-cost resources that will help them pay for housing and transportation.
4. For parents needing legal services, facilitate access to affordable immigration and naturalization support.
5. Target extra wraparound support and resources to campuses with high rates of need, specifically the newcomer immigrant-serving campuses.
6. Ensure information on wraparound services and other supports are

---

8. See the HERC summary publication by Camila Cigarroa Kennedy and Kori Stroub, "Recommendations Based on Results from the 2021–22 HISD Student Needs Survey," Houston Education Research Consortium, Kinder Institute for Urban Research, Rice University, November 2022, https://tinyurl.com/mtur2j6d.

available in Spanish. Prioritize language support for parents as well as students.

Here, then, are targeted areas—student mobility, English as a second language, funding equity, and wraparound needs—in which you can work to make changes that will improve the educational success of students. Look first for an organization already working on such changes, and join it. If none exists, consider starting one with others to work for such changes.

Third, and importantly, we must consider access to college. The current system is financially challenging. A college degree costs an incredible amount of money. Many cannot afford it. Too many end up with massive student loan debt, greatly restricting what they can do post-college, as they must focus on repaying loans over the next ten years of their life.

Consider this: as a society we have agreed that from kindergarten through high school, education should be provided to the student for free. We do so by taxing adults, whether they have children or not. We do this because we have come to view such education as a right, a necessity, and a responsibility of the citizenry. In many nations, education at any level is provided for free through taxation, not just K–12.

Due to the increases in education needed for the modern economy and world, a college degree is now the new high school diploma. We can work for kingdom racial change with a very focused goal: create a new educational act that (a) provides for free college education for all citizens and residents and (b) provides the funding mechanism to do so. We already have the blueprint from K–12 education and from other nations that provide free education through college or beyond. Such change is desperately needed and can have a significant impact on reducing racial and economic injustice. As the Kinder Institute at Rice University puts it, we should seek inclusive prosperity, where everyone can contribute to the nation's success and share in its opportunities.

The 3 Rs—Repentance, Reparations, and Repair

The Bible teaches us we were born sinners. This seems entirely unfair. Before we have made a single decision or even engaged in a single action, we are guilty of sin. And that sin has but one ending: permanent death (hell). No wonder lots of people reject the Christian message outright. It is patently anti-American, and it is anti-humanist. According to Christian teaching, we are not the captains of our ship. The Christian reality is that we are exactly as we are born—helpless and 100 percent dependent on another for survival. We need a Christ. Without Jesus, we live a few decades pursuing meaninglessness and then return to dust. What difference does it make if we have a lot of education or likes on social media or if people think we are successful? All those people die, too, and even the most remembered people to ever live are just names and dates to memorize for a history test.

Though we are tempted to be swept into the world's meaninglessness, believers have a different code, a different and lasting purpose. We are to glorify God. Jesus says, "If you love me, keep my commands" (John 14:15). Books can be written on analyzing Jesus's commands, but one of them that he and his followers highlight is his new command: love another. This command is crystal clear. Love another.

Loving another does not mean letting others do what they want (tolerance, acceptance). The world seems to think this is what love is, but such a definition of love has zero resemblance to Christian love. Christian love is something closer to the love we have for our children. Because we love our children, we sacrifice for them. We would die for them. We also tell our children no (often, it seems) to keep them from harm, to instruct them in the ways they should go. We teach them to move away from self-centeredness. We teach them to care about the needs of others. Christian love is other-centeredness. When fully practiced, it is the beloved community. It is full of conflict, to be sure, but it never gives up; it doesn't quit, and it will do what it can to reconcile and repair (see 1 Cor. 13).

Let's consider a practical example. A brother and sister, close in age, generally got along well as they grew up. Sure, they had their share of spats, but they got past them typically fairly quickly. That is until *that day*, as it came to be called. The brother "borrowed" his sister's most prized possession without asking. Not only that, but he took it with him to school on that day. It was there that he misplaced it, and when he eventually found it, it had been destroyed.

When the sister discovered her most prized possession was missing, she was horrified. Where could it be? She searched high and low, first in her room, then throughout the house, the garage, and the yard, and she even called friends whose homes she had recently visited. It was nowhere to be found.

She went to her brother. Had he seen it? He decided it would be easier to lie that he had not rather than try to explain what had happened to it.

This possession meant so much to his sister that she spent the next several days in her room in tears and depression, refusing to eat or attend school. Her parents became worried. They got involved in investigating what had happened. They eventually found out that the brother had taken the possession.

After much talk, they told the brother he must confess to his sister and make things right so that she could return to living life normally. The brother dragged his feet for several days. The parents put more pressure on him, eventually threatening to ground him for a significant time and to take away his own prized possession.

Finally, the brother knocked on the sister's bedroom door, asking if he could come in. His sister, now in a state of listless depression, said in a barely audible voice, "Whatever you want."

The brother came in and sat at the foot of her bed. "Sis, I can't stand to see you like this. It isn't you. And it is because of me. I have done a horrible thing. Two weeks ago, I took your most prized possession without asking. I took it to school to show my friends, but I misplaced it somehow. When I finally found it, it had been crushed. I am so sorry for what I have done. It was stupid, it was wrong, it was unchristian, and it was not something I should have ever done, let alone to my own sister. Can you forgive me?"

With the brother's apology, the onus is now on the sister. She has to make a choice. She has been told what happened, learned who did it, and is now being asked to forgive and, in this sense, to move on, to forget, and to get back to normal.

The reality is that none of us—if we had a truly prized possession and had it taken from us by someone we trusted to love us—could immediately forgive and forget. We would need to ask questions, we would want to express our feelings (outrage, hurt) about what this person had done to us, and we would need time to work through it all.

But to do any of that, we would need our brother to promise he would never do such a thing again, and we would need him to find a way to replace the prized possession. Could we forgive and forget if he refused to do these two actions? Could the sister regain trust in her brother? The short answer is no.

If the brother is truly sorry and loves his sister, it is clear to us what he must do—replace the prized possession and never do it again. Standing on the outside, we can easily see the right course of action. But if we were the brother, would we see it as clearly? Or would we look for justifications not to do what the sister is asking? After all, the prized possession is gone. It cannot simply be replaced by buying another because it was a one-of-a-kind. Shouldn't the sister just not be as materialistic? Why won't she forgive? Why is she demanding more than an apology?

Anyone reading this book knows where we are headed with this story. Entire peoples' humanity and possessions have been repeatedly taken, and the best we have had to offer thus far is, "So sorry, can you forgive?" And then we say in so many words, "Move on."

As we seek to be Jesus's followers, as we seek to be other-centered, as we seek to love one another, we must repent and repair, and this will involve reparations (to replace the prized possession), a specific kind that we will discuss. We are drawing directly on *Rebirth of a Nation* (2024), written by Joel Goza.[9] Goza spent years reading writings on how healing happens, and the result is his book, which draws on the wisdom of the top thinkers on the topic. We will summarize here, but we recommend reading the full book for full understanding. He focuses on a three-step process of repentance, repayment, and repair.

As in our story of the brother and sister above, we cannot have kingdom racial change without confronting the wrongs that have been done to people groups. This is difficult because it is group to group rather than person to person; it involves not just now but the past; it requires people willing to admit wrong was done and that they are accountable or have unfairly reaped the advantages of those wrongs; it requires other people groups to forgive; and it involves the complexity of what groups we are talking about. Given these factors, we quickly devolve into pointing fingers with the same end result for hundreds of years: no repentance.

But short of finding a way for truth and reconciliation (the term South Africa used for its repentance forums), we will never have true kingdom racial change, just as being short of admitting we have sinned and are in

---

9. Joel Goza, *Rebirth of a Nation: Reparations and Remaking America* (Grand Rapids: Eerdmans, 2024).

need of a savior (repentance) will leave us spiritually doomed. As Goza writes: *"Repentance is the soul work required to re-create our society."*[10]

Repentance is not white guilt. It is not a forced "sorry." Repentance is a complete turning from a past and present, saying in words and actions that grave wrongs have been done, prized possessions have been stolen, and this will happen no more. The prized possessions will be returned or replaced (reparations), and no longer shall people gain rewards or suffer costs because of their skin color.

But how? Repentance focuses on the accountability of the violators and the dignity of the violated. This must be done communally because it is a national, macro-level problem. The scale of the solution must match the scale of the problem. Goza outlines the ingredients needed to create kingdom racial repentance: (1) it must occur within minority-led spaces (the brother came to his sister's room rather than ask her to come to his space); (2) we must come to define ourselves and our collective understanding not by the economic, political, and social winners, but by the least of these, exactly as Jesus taught us; and (3) we must engage in penitent politics. As racial inequality has been encoded in laws, policies, procedures, and political structures, penitent politics is about reforging "a racist past into a reparative future." Racially biased laws must be remade into laws "with liberty and justice for all." Such work will require social movements—some of which are already underway through the leading of organizations (for example, The Equal Justice Initiative, which we recommend getting involved in), and some yet remain to be started. We shall outline in the next chapter the steps toward a successful social movement.

And now the explosive word: *reparations* (what Goza calls *repayment*). Want to start a fight? Want to get white Americans quickly cursing? Just say you think we as a nation should consider reparations. We found in our research that the mere mention of this word puts many white people (and some others) on the strong defensive. Blood pressures increase, spoken tones become sharper and more direct, and in our studies the single most commonly expressed feeling—especially among white Christians—was anger.

What is angering about the word *reparations*? It goes something like this: either there has never been a reason for such a thing or there is no longer a reason. Everybody has an equal opportunity to make some-

---

10. Goza, *Rebirth of a Nation*, 240; emphasis in the original.

Part 2. Making Kingdom Racial Change

thing of themselves. Making reparations is stealing money from a group of people who worked hard for it and giving it to people who don't deserve it. It is theft. Who would receive reparations anyway? And why am I, a modern American, being asked to give away my money for possible wrongs done centuries ago? It makes no sense. So enough with such nonsense. Get over it.

As we consider ourselves as Christians, not Americans or some other nationality, race, or identity group, nothing in the above paragraph is Christ-like, the very goal we are professing to when we profess to be Christians. We are not writing this book to convince people who do not believe we have racial injustice. We are writing to Christians looking to be part of kingdom racial change.

Just as the brother in our story, to reconcile with his sister, had to find a way to make amends for the prized possession, so we as Christians will be driven to do so across the racial chasms. As we saw in the first portion of this book, our current realities are destructive to some Christians while at the same time a huge benefit for others. Jesus weeps. As Joel Goza writes, "Until we stand ready to pay for our racial crimes, we stand ready to repeat them," and reparations are "a merciful way to tend to our nation's self-inflicted wounds" on persons of color.[11]

But reparations—or repayment—is such a big concept. And truly, how would it happen? Thanks to the amazing work of many others, making reparations is not as complicated as we might think. Focusing just on Black Americans, scholars William Darity and A. Kristen Mullen in their powerful book, *From Here to Equality*, argue the clearest, best measure of reparations is the racial wealth gap. It provides a direct measure of the cumulative economic advantage white privilege has afforded white folks across the generations. The current racial wealth gap is substantial, standing at a $357,000 deficit per Black American relative to white Americans. The total required across all Black Americans? $14.3 trillion. This massive sum represents four hundred years of racial oppression, illegally garnishing wealth for one group from another.

The calculation is straightforward, but how would the nation ever be able to pay $14.3 trillion, let alone support such a payment? Again, it is not as complicated or far a reach as we might think.[12] First, many

---

11. Goza, *Rebirth of a Nation*, 260–61.
12. See William A. Darity and A. Kirsten Mullen, *From Here to Equality: Repara-*

scholars on this topic recommend that payments occur over ten years, meaning payments of $35,700 per African American per year for a decade (or held in trusts for those under eighteen). Second, while there are many routes to produce this money, after substantial investigation, Goza recommends the following, a method that most of us may not consider:

> In a land that deprived millions of Black people of equitable education, housing, and health care, the radical accumulation of white wealth was never a victimless crime. And we stand at a point in history where the most feasible way of righting this historical wrong is to return inheritance taxes on the wealthiest families to their pre-Reagan levels.[13]

To the inheritance tax rate, Goza adds the estate tax exemption. We will note here why these both matter. If their rates were returned to what they had been for decades before they were changed in the 1980s, enough money for reparations would easily be achieved. Such a recommendation has the incredible advantage that it asks nothing of poorer folks of any hue.

The wealth people gain in each generation is passed on to the next generation. Because white people have, on average, ten to twenty times the wealth of others, being able to pass on that wealth at low tax rates results in accumulating white wealth advantage across time, increasing the racial wealth disparities across each subsequent generation. When Ronald Reagan was president (1980–1988), massive amounts of white wealth were due to be transferred to the next generation. But such wealth transfers were taxed. Those tax rates were reduced during Reagan's first term as president from a maximum of 70 percent, which had been the maximum rate since 1935, to 55 percent by 1984 (and as of this writing, the maximum rate has further been reduced to just 40 percent).

As a result, a far higher amount and percentage of wealth could be passed on to the next generation. As of this writing, that generation is now preparing to pass an estimated nearly $70 trillion on to the next

---

tions for Black Americans in the Twenty-First Century, 2nd ed. (Chapel Hill: University of North Carolina Press, 2022).

13. Goza, *Rebirth of a Nation*, 262.

generation. Notice this amount of $70 trillion. It is mind-boggling, as it is *five times greater* than the cumulative calculation of what is owed to African Americans for four hundred years of theft.

This is the reason why, if the inheritance tax and estate tax exemption were to revert to the pre-Reagan era, enough funds would result to return to African Americans what has been taken from them.

Let's break this down. In 1979, the year before Reagan began his presidency, the estate tax exemption was $147,000. This means that for the first $147,000 of wealth transfer, no tax was levied. If we account for inflation and this tax exemption level had not changed at the time of this writing, it would mean no tax on the first $588,000 of wealth as it is passed on to the next generation.

However, we noted the exemption was changed so the wealthy and very wealthy could pass on more of their wealth. In today's money, was the exemption increased from $473,000 to $1 million? Perhaps $2 million? Not close. The actual estate exemption now stands at $13.61 million. Are you married? The tax exemption doubles to $27.22 million.

Amazing. More than $27 million can be passed on to the next generation tax-free. It is no wonder that the wealth of the richest families has increased during these past forty-five years by a seemingly unbelievable 1,007 percent.[14] Does this much money need to be passed on tax-free? Could the children of the wealthy still thrive if only the first $1 million were not taxed, whereas the rest were taxed? Surely, they would still be receiving substantial amounts of money, which, truth be told, they did not earn.

If two revisions to the tax code were made—reduce the estate tax exemption to $1 million and increase the maximum tax rate back to what it was from 1935 to 1981 (70 percent)—we would not only produce enough funds for reparations but would have overflow to be used to correct injustices continually. Reparations will lead in good part to the repair of broken promises, repair of broken relationships, and repair of macro structures designed to be unfair.

In sum, Goza and the works he draws on show how these repayments to African Americans would make substantial change, kingdom racial change, and be part of the repair process. The details often brought up—such as whether it is fair to tax the passing on of

---

14. Robin Kaiser-Schatzlein, "This Is How America's Richest Families Stay That Way," *New York Times*, September 24, 2021.

Make No Small Plans—Macro-Level Change

wealth and who would qualify for reparations payments—we will not explore here, as other works explore such details. If you are drawn to be part of this change, such questions you can most certainly find answers to.

Conclusion

In Isaiah 58 God's people were complaining to God. We have fasted, they told God, but you don't see it. We have humbled ourselves, they told God, but you don't notice. What is up with that? When will our prayers be answered?

God's reply is striking. The Lord says to his people, in essence, that their perceived righteousness is self-deception. God notes that his people claim they are humbling themselves and fasting, yet on their fast days, they do what they please, they exploit the workers, they quarrel, and they fight. The Lord continues:

> Is that what you call fast, a day acceptable to the Lord? Is not this the kind of fasting I have chosen: to loose the chains of injustice and untie the cords of the yoke, to set the oppressed free and break every yoke? Is it not to share your food with the hungry and to provide the poor wanderer with shelter—when you see the naked, to clothe them, and not to turn away from your own flesh and blood? (Isa. 58:5b–7)

We think of fasting as not eating. God has something else in mind, and it is macro-level justice work. The Lord chooses working for kingdom change as authentic fasting, as well as moving from inequality and unjust systems and relationships to just ones. In short, God is asking that we fast not from food but from self. Fasting brings us to the realization that we must be other-centered, focused on the call to join God in making things right in the world.

These verses become all the more amazing when we consider Jesus announcing his public ministry. In the synagogue, he stood up and read from the scroll of Isaiah:

> The Spirit of the Sovereign Lord is on me, because the Lord has anointed me to proclaim good news to the poor. He has sent me to bind up the brokenhearted, to proclaim freedom for the captives and

release from darkness for the prisoners, to proclaim the year of the Lord's favor . . . (Isa. 61:1-2)

And then, after sitting back down with all eyes focused on him, he said: "Today this scripture is fulfilled in your hearing" (Luke 4:21). Jesus's ministry and very identity exactly align with who God asks his people to be in true fasting. In announcing who he was, Jesus said nothing about what education he had, what credentials made him important, what neighborhood he lived in, or even what influential people he knew. His identity and purpose had nothing to do with any such things. Rather, he was completely other-centered, sent to restore justice, freedom, and sight and bring good news. As Christians who are called to be Christ-like, our model is clear.

Macro change for kingdom racial change is essential. Without it, racial inequality will not only continue but increase with each generation. Oppression increases, and yokes grow heavier. None of us, as individuals or small groups or single churches, can do macro change. Macro change requires a macro movement, culminating in changes in laws, practices, regulations, and beliefs.

Thus, macro-level changes—compared to meso-level and micro-level changes—are the most difficult to make. So most of us avoid trying. And others of us, if we try, not seeing the change we hope for, eventually give up and move on. Yet we are called to something much more.

Recall the three building blocks for macro change: (1) The mighty arm of racial power is that it is systemic. It is not that prejudice exists, or that some people discriminate against others that causes such severe racial injustice. No, the true power of racial injustice is that it is sewn deeply into systems, laws, and practices. (2) We must overcome the link between race and class, for this link is destructive and a lie. And (3) we must directly address whatever creates inequality between God's people. Given (3), we need to address (1) and (2). This chapter has proposed specific ways to do so.

We have discussed three areas in desperate need of macro-level change that will have a substantial impact in bringing about kingdom racial change. We have focused on the housing industry, the educational system, and the *R*s: repentance, reparations, and repair.[15]

---

15. We discuss three macro-level areas for kingdom racial change. There are others, such as reforming the criminal-justice system. See, for example, Domi-

Make No Small Plans—Macro-Level Change

Pick one and only one to focus on. Staying focused and committed for the long term is essential. Trust that God will call others to address areas different than that which you are focusing on. To decide which of the three to focus upon, pray for direction, and notice which area you feel most drawn to, have the most connections for, or have the most passion about.

Once you select an area, then what? Macro-level change requires meso-level social movements. Such movements may mean marching in the streets or supporting an organization already working for the macro change. In the next chapter, we will explore not only how meso-level change can occur but the characteristics of successful social movements. What makes them work, whereas most fail? We shall soon find out.

---

nique Gilliard, *Rethinking Incarceration: Advocating for Restorative Justice* (Downers Grove, IL: InterVarsity Press, 2018).

6

The Meso-Level Change Levers

Macro change is, by definition, huge! None of us can make such a change as individuals or small groups. So, even if we want to make such a change, we are stuck. Yet, actually, we are not!

The meso level of social life—such as churches, schools, places of employment, social networks of relationships, and coordinated social movements of people—is the level at which most of our social life occurs. And it is precisely at this level that we can make change, both at the meso and macro levels. As Peter Block, an expert in organizational development, community building, and civic engagement who trains clergy and others for change, writes in his book *Community: The Structure of Belonging*, "Relationships are the foundation . . . [but] it is only by embedding them in robust social structures [that social life] can be substantially improved."[1] That is to say, while we all value our relationships and live most of life within the context of those relationships, it is at the meso level that those relationships are organized, shaped, and given direction and meaning. Hence, it is at the meso level—the level that ties together our micro-level relationships and the macro-level institutions discussed in the previous chapter—that kingdom racial change gets its energy and power.

This chapter will focus on the three central meso-level realities—organizations, social networks, and social movements—which are the social structures that embed and animate our relationships. This trilogy of meso-level realities captures the meso-level building blocks we identified in the first four chapters:

1. Peter Block, *Community: The Structure of Belonging* (Oakland, CA: Berrett-Koehler, 2018), 5.

The Meso-Level Change Levers

1. We must understand Black advantages just as much as white advantages (Building Block 3).
2. We have an urgent and essential need to root out the Religion of Whiteness from religious communities. Doing so is a fundamental requirement in our path toward God's family (Building Block 4).
3. We, as Christians, have a fantastic opportunity to change the structure of networks and connections (who and how). God tells us our primary identity is that we are his children. Fellow Christians are, by definition, our siblings. We are to help one another. As Christians, we were empowered to overcome divisions in our communities. God has given us the path (Building Block 7).
4. When God puts you in a position to help others of different racial groups thrive, do so (Building Block 8).
5. Significant change often occurs through social movements, which themselves occur through community organization and group cooperation (Building Block 11).

In short, whereas chapter 5 identified needed key macro-level changes, this chapter shows us how to go about those changes. It also shows us how to make meso-level changes, such as in our churches. In the end, kingdom racial change comes *by participating in Christian community through social networks, organizations, and social movements.*

The prelude of this book introduced you briefly to the Unity Men's Group stemming from Chicagoland (the name for the Chicago metropolitan area of about ten million people) and founded by Dr. David and Rev. Ev. The group represents a clear example of operating at the meso-level. It started as a social network of relationships among African American men, then it expanded across racial lines. An organization, Unity in the Church, was formed to nurture and develop those relationships and have a larger impact beyond the relationships. A social movement will be its next stage to reach its goals.

To understand how social networks, organizations, and social movements are the key to kingdom racial change, let's explore the path of this organization as it has and continues to develop. Keep in mind that although Unity in the Church, at the time of this writing, is primarily localized and limited to men, what it illustrates is not bound by place, gender, or age.

Part 2. Making Kingdom Racial Change

The Illustrative Story of Unity in the Church

When Dr. David and his wife moved back to Chicago after completing his medical training, they returned to his childhood church. The church had a men's group that met monthly for breakfast and Bible study, involving perhaps a dozen men. Dr. David hungered for more. He talked with Rev. Ev. They decided to plan additional events for the men, such as sporting events and religious conferences. Based on the feedback and growing attendance, these additional gatherings went over well with the men. At this point, the men were all African American. Soon, as word spread through their social networks, other Black churches began bringing men to the gatherings. Before they knew it, about one hundred African American men were participating. Dr. David and Rev. Ev. decided to dream big, planning to ultimately have one thousand black men attend the annual Chicago White Sox–Cubs Crosstown Classic baseball game. At these games—with the Christian-programmed tailgating beforehand—and the other gatherings, emphasis was placed on creating friendships and a supportive social network to encourage one another to live godly lives.

During the planning time for the expansion of the network, as Dr. David drove home from making his hospital rounds, he heard God speak to him. It was a strangely specific and trajectory-altering call. Dr. David heard God say, "Give Willow Creek Church [the well-known suburban, largely white megachurch] twenty tickets to the next Crosstown Classic." The call took Dr. David aback. At first, he resisted, but he soon realized he wanted to be obedient despite the risk of doing so, given that it would mean inviting a very different group of men than were currently part of the group.

He called Rev. Ev. and shared what God had said. Rev. Ev. was understandably skeptical. "Is that really what God said? Just when the group is going so well, now we are going to risk it all by inviting white men to the group?" He continued to express that such an invitation could go very poorly along several fronts: how the white men would perceive the African American men; the possibility of the Black men dropping out; and, as they had seen repeatedly in their lives, the high probability of the white men "taking over" so things would be done their way, including putting strong limits on talking about racial issues. Rev. Ev. was straight-up honest. He told Dr. David that, as a person in the flesh, he was against this idea. But, ultimately, as a Christian, he would be obedient if this were of God.

They next turned to asking the opinion of the other men involved in the network. A significant majority were against inviting men from Willow Creek for the same reasons expressed by Rev. Ev. Despite this feedback and the significant risk to the continuation of the network, Dr. David, with the support of Rev. Ev., determined he had to take the step of faith and invite men from Willow Creek to the gathering.

With the decision made, a group of Black men went to Willow Creek to invite twenty Willow Creek men to the Crosstown Classic. To "flip" the common narrative of poor Black men and well-to-do white men, Dr. David told Willow Creek that the Black men's network would be paying for the tickets and would provide the tailgating food. The Willow Creek men need only attend and participate. Importantly, note also that in this case Black men were leading the network and extending an invitation to white men. In so doing, they were drawing upon what we discussed in chapter 2 as Black advantages—having more and deeper social relationship bonds, being more involved in religious networks, and being more likely to be religiously committed.

The representatives at Willow Creek were hesitant. What was this group? Why were they being asked to attend? After getting questions answered, though, they accepted the offer. The date and time were set.

On the day of the game, the Black men came to the tailgate about two hours early to prepare the food and arrange the seating. They were fully ready to debunk the stereotype they feared the Willow Creek men would hold of them, that Black folks are late and unprepared. When the men of Willow Creek arrived, the Black men hugged and welcomed them. Even with the hugs, the Black men were concerned whether this "experiment" could work or if it would backfire. But as Dr. David said:

> After about fifteen minutes of watching the Black and white men engage, I noticed that something was different. Very different. Whatever charisma, excitement, and anointing that the Black men generated when we met within our Black network, what I was experiencing on this day was ten times as great. I was floored! Once again, God knew all along what he was doing. He knew there is power in unity, especially between such a divided people. Michael, myself, and the leaders of the Willow Creek men realized we must continue this

multiracial fellowship and that we must break down the walls that constrain us.

That first gathering, fraught with fear, uncertainty, and distrust, quickly did a complete turn. The men were energized. All involved realized it was but one gathering, and the real tests would be down the road. Yet, they were hopeful. They were hopeful because the gathering exceeded what they imagined possible. It felt as if God was indeed behind this growing network, soon to be an organization and a movement. At this gathering, therefore, the men committed to join together again at the next Crosstown Classic. Willow Creek went so far as to designate a person to meet with Dr. David and Rev. Ev. to plan the next Crosstown Classic and other events.

During the first meeting of Dr. David, Rev. Ev, and Willow Creek's appointed leader, they determined that a retreat for spiritual growth and creating a broader and deeper network of friendships was needed. A planning team was soon created for that very purpose, meeting monthly to plan the retreat for May 2020. An out-of-state location was identified, and a significant deposit was made to secure it.

But when the COVID-19 pandemic hit, Dr. David wanted to postpone the retreat to August, to reduce the possibility of spreading the virus. The Willow Creek leader disagreed. He also disagreed that racial reconciliation should be discussed at the retreat, stating that white men were tired of the topic. He felt so strongly in his views that he took back his portion of the retreat deposit and left the network. With that action, the other white men of the planning group left as well.

Here it was. The moment that the Black men not only feared but expected. White men, not agreeing, simply walk away rather than find a solution that furthers the group. And now the entire group and the planned gatherings were at risk.

With just the three Black men (Rev. Ev., Dr. David, and Dr. David's son) remaining on the planning committee, they decided they must move forward with what they understood to be God's call. They funded the entirety of the retreat deposit as an expression of that faith.

A new, stronger, diversified planning team was created with three men from Willow Creek—two white, one Asian—and Rev. Ev. and Dr. David. These men developed strong bonds, including sharing meals with one another's families and even vacationing together.

Because the pandemic continued to rage, the Crosstown Classic was canceled, and the first conference was moved to Zoom. The planning team worked together to make these decisions. They also determined they would indeed talk about racial reconciliation.

With the move to Zoom, the planning team designed a quarterly virtual gathering featuring well-known speakers and group discussion and prayer rather than one marathon session. Up to 250 men from a range of racial and other backgrounds attended the Zoom sessions.

But during that peak of attendance, an intense conversation on racial injustice and racial reconciliation occurred. Men spoke their minds. From that point, the attendance of white men declined. Clearly, establishing an interracial social network would be a battle. The team committed to prayer, fasting, patience, and endurance.

Eventually, the first in-person conference was held in a nearby state. About 150 men attended, far more than expected. After the conference, the men attended the Crosstown Classic together. At this point, the group also connected with a Hispanic church, which sent men to the game as well. This church now regularly brings fifty Hispanic men to the gatherings.

As the planning team sought to find additional ways to create deep interracial bonds, two multiracial groups were developed, meeting monthly. They also developed pulpit exchanges, with pastors and their congregation going to another group's church. These exchanges have been high points in the journey, being exceedingly popular among the participants. Additionally, the group "adopted" a grade school in the Chicago south side neighborhood where Dr. David attends church. The multiracial group of men have gathered at the school and, with permission, have walked the hallways and classrooms praying for the students, teachers, and staff.

With the social network's growing numbers, complexity, and aims, the planning team moved to formalize the group into an organization, calling it Unity in the Church (UnityInTheChurch.org). The mission of this organization is to explore equity, brotherhood, and friendship across racial lines. Notice that its mission has micro-level goals (friendships), meso-level goals (cross-race social networks and unity within and across churches), and macro-level goals (working for racial equity and reconciliation).

Creating an organization formalized the group's expanding social network, brought clarity to its purposes, and created structure and resources to achieve its goals. These are the exact same reasons any organization is created. Consider churches. The early church, meeting in homes, was originally an interconnected set of social networks. But as the social networks expanded, the early believers organized and formalized into a church to continue with the work of God. Visions and missions must be formally stated, a leadership structure must be created, membership rules need to be set, and beliefs and practices must be made clear in the face of competing views. Local churches—religious organizations—then work with pooled resources, directing those resources where needed, such as meal trains, discipleship programs, supporting pastors and missionaries, and the like. Social networks lack such abilities (for example, they lack clear goals, authority structures, and often pooled resources), so they usually eventually organize into organizations.

The Central Role of Organizations

Drawing on the work of sociologist Victor Ray and others, we note that organizations are the key cogs in the larger, macro-level racial system.[2] This is because organizations (think churches, schools, workplaces, and more) are the sites where resources are found, accessed, and used, be they financial, social, psychological, or religious resources. Organizations—which have structure, rules, and often memberships—shape access to resources and empower or constrain the agency of people and groups.

Because of our American history, organizations are overwhelmingly racialized. That is to say, organizations function to reify racial differences and inequality. They often do so unintentionally. They simply function in ways that assume whiteness or Blackness or Asianness and so on. This is the case whether the organization is uniracial or multiracial. Unfortunately, demographic diversity does *not* equal justice, reconciliation, or unity. Demographic diversity is more typically an addendum, an add-on of people expected to conform to the organization's existing beliefs, practices, and structures. For example, within churches, the preaching style and sermon topics, more often than not, remain the same even if a church demographically diversifies. What

2. Victor Ray, "A Theory of Racialized Organizations," *American Sociological Review* 84, no. 1 (2019): 26–53.

is more, the music typically remains the same at the core, despite an occasional add-on of a song in another language or style. Who gets held up as role models, appointed to leadership positions, and the like all overwhelmingly reify racialization. As sociologist Korie Little Edwards finds in her work, even if, for example, a diversifying formally white church appoints a pastor of another racial background, that person will be expected—in truth, required—to conform to white norms of a particular seminary education, beliefs, styles of preaching, topics that can be discussed, practices, and social networks.[3]

So, the irony is that the very places that can produce monumental kingdom racial change—organizations—are the very places that do exactly the opposite. Want to contribute to change? Let's stop making racial and ethnic diversity the goal and instead make them a means to the goals of justice, reconciliation, and unity. To do that requires (a) thinking about the means and the goals differently and (b) focusing on the processes of justice, reconciliation, and unity. Fortunately, several good books already exist to help us do exactly that. Do an internet search to find the latest books.

We must note, though, that the highest hurdle to overcome is what we noted in chapter 2, the Religion of Whiteness. To fully understand this religion, we recommend the book *The Religion of Whiteness*,[4] but let us summarize what it is. Since all religion specifies what is sacred—and how we should believe and act toward the sacred—and what is profane, the Religion of Whiteness (ROW) is defined as a *unified system of beliefs and practices that worships and sacralizes whiteness while declaring profane things not associated with whiteness*. Whiteness is defined simply as white people (along with supporters of other hues) and their dominance. It is that imagined right to dominance and rightness that empowers its followers to declare, for example, that the Unity Men's group will not talk about racial reconciliation, because white people don't want to. Within the context of the ROW (the Religion of Whiteness), that is all the reason needed.

The ROW deeply distorts and twists many Christian churches. By our empirical estimates, a full two-thirds of white practicing Christians are also followers of the ROW. While they attempt to worship the true

---

3. Korie Little Edwards, *The Elusive Dream: The Power of Race in Interracial Churches*, updated version (New York: Oxford University Press, 2021).
4. Emerson and Bracey, *Religion of Whiteness*.

Part 2. Making Kingdom Racial Change

God, that worship and their relationships with others are profoundly clouded by this other religion, the ROW, which directs them to place on equal or higher footing the worship of whiteness. The ROW is defended even at the cost of broken cross-racial friendships, social networks, and organizations. This damage is justified in the name of staying true to the authentic faith, "sticking to the gospel," and defending the faith against heretics. The problem is the ROW is the heretic, is inauthentic, and has departed far from the gospel.

As such, for kingdom racial change, *the ROW must go*. As Christ says, "If a house is divided against itself, that house will not stand" (Mark 3:25 ESV). In this context, we can take that to mean that if a church attempts to co-host Christians and ROW followers, it will fail. Jesus goes further, saying in the previous verse, "If a kingdom is divided against itself, that kingdom cannot stand" (Mark 3:24 ESV). Want kingdom racial change? The ROW must go. Its presence cuts Christendom off at the knees.

How shall we root out this uninvited religion from our churches? Consider GPS, which is now so prevalent in our travels that we often don't know how to get somewhere without it. When we make a wrong turn or completely miss a needed turn, the GPS doesn't panic, give up, curse at us, or cry. It simply says, "Recalculating," and it creates a new path. It can do so because the destination is clear.

The church as a whole and many local churches have made wrong turns and missed needed turns, such that the ROW has taken them off course. We must recalculate by doing the following:

1. **Name the need to recalculate because we have gotten off course**. The ROW has taken many a church off its stated Christian mission and harmed the Christian community. With neither anger nor malice, name the reality—the ROW must go.
2. **Make clear the destination**. What is a Christian community? What is our calling as the church? In short, what is our destination? (We explore these questions in the next section.)
3. **Address betrayal trauma**. Betrayal trauma is the deep collateral damage that the ROW leaves in its wake. For social life to work, we must trust. Trust is the liquid gold of life within our Christian communities. When organizations and the people in them significantly violate that trust, it deeply injures people. Many a person has left the faith because of the resultant betrayal trauma. As we work to root out the ROW, we must tend to the wounded.

4. **Map a new path.** Despite having gone off course, when we reclaim the clarity of our destination and tend to our wounded, we are ready to recalculate our route. This will involve the necessity of teaching against the ROW and encouraging ROW followers to either leave the ROW faith or leave the Christian congregation. For many white congregations, in particular, it will mean a reenvisioning of the path to our destination, such as outlined in the book *Rediscipling the White Church*.[5]

5. **Coordinate ministry.** The mission to root out the ROW and work for kingdom racial change is necessarily massive. God is big! We are called to work for the mission together. Though separate creeks want to flow in their own directions, we are called to conjoin into one mighty river of justice, reconciliation, and unity as we flow to our singular destination of God and heaven. This is why we need a social movement (explored later in the chapter), campaigning for the ROW to go and for the beauty of the Christian community to be strengthened.

What Christian Community Is and Isn't

Kingdom racial change hinges on Christian community. Many a Christian leader through the centuries has taught on Christian community. Dietrich Bonhoeffer, a martyr for the faith during World War II, has long been respected for his dedication to the Christian community and for the ultimate sacrifice he made for it. He notes well something we, as the authors, have seen in our own lives as we attempt to live within the Christian community. Writing in a time when the use of "he" and "man" were the global references to all people, Bonhoeffer shared these astute observations in his book *Life Together*:

> Innumerable times a whole Christian community has broken down because it has sprung from a wish dream . . . a very definite idea of what Christian life together should be. . . . But God's grace speedily shatters such dreams.
>
> He who loves his dream of a community more than the Christian

---

5. David W. Swanson, *Rediscipling the White Church: From Cheap Diversity to True Solidarity* (Downers Grove, IL: InterVarsity Press, 2020).

community itself becomes a destroyer of the latter, even though his personal intentions may be ever so honest and earnest and sacrificial.

The man who fashions a visionary ideal of community demands that it be realized by God, by others, and by himself. He enters the community of Christians with his demands, sets up his own law, and judges the brethren and God Himself accordingly. When things do not go their way, they call the effort a failure. He becomes an accuser of his brethren, then an accuser of God, and finally the despairing accuser of himself.

Because God has already laid the only foundation of our fellowship, because God has bound us together in one body with other Christians in Jesus Christ, long before we entered into common life with them, we enter into this common life not as demanders, but as thankful recipients.

Christian brotherhood is not an ideal which we must realize; it is rather a reality created by God in Christ in which we may participate.[6]

Let us take note of the wisdom in these quotes. Christian community is comprised of broken but redeemed people purchased by Christ. We are brought together in community by Christ, our singular commonality. We don't demand what this diverse community is to be or look like; we give praise that we have been called to participate in it.

We have one legitimate, biblical challenge we can make within the Christian community—we can expect us all to be Christ's followers, that those in the community are indeed called there. We don't have the right to change people to all be nice or use deodorant; we do, though, have the responsibility to collectively keep out that which is not Christ, such as the ROW. The ROW can have its place, but it is not within Christian communities.

In Christian community, we support one another in following Christ. We may have visions of what we want the Christian community to be—such as everyone dances, or no one dances—but the wisdom here is we must let go of such visions and expectations. We are brought together by Christ. We participate in supporting and discipling one another no matter our differences, quirks, or irritating behaviors. The food of the Christian community is grace, always giving one another the benefit of the doubt, and always assuming the best intentions of fellow Christians.

---

6. From Bonhoeffer, *Life Together*, 26–30.

When we have deep disagreements in our community, here is what does not work: sitting down and trying to work it out. What does work? Action, as in working together for a common goal, serving together. In the process, we come to admire one another, and we have created a basis to work through disagreements. This is why the very process of working for kingdom racial change together can be community strengthening and an opportunity for spiritual growth.

How to Engage in Social Movements for Kingdom Racial Change

If an organization's goals are internal—such as supporting its members—it can focus on the group itself. But far more often, an organization seeks to have influence beyond its borders, be that changing related organizations, expanding its social networks through proselytizing and ministry, or, in the case of this book, realizing kingdom racial change.

And to do that, the "magic" potion is a social movement. A social movement is a collective effort of social networks and organizations campaigning to prevent or make meso-level and macro-level changes. It takes a good deal of coordination and intention for a social movement to be successful. Still, by studying those that have been successful, we can identify the eight main components of successful social movements, where "success" means the movement's goals were largely realized.

Successful social movements have eight characteristics in common. Here they are:

1. **Clearly identify the problem and the solution**. The problem may be specific—the presence of the ROW in Christian churches—or broader—racial inequality within society. Regardless, the problem and its consequences must be specified, or there is no way to find a solution. Many attempts at social movements fail at this step, offering only a vague complaint about something. Or, perhaps even more commonly, they identify the problem but have no clear solution. This is akin to knowing you don't like your current job but having no idea what to do about it. You end up simply looking like a complainer. Time must be spent studying the problem and outlining a solution.
2. **Show institutional failure**. This step is an interesting one. For meso- or macro-level change, a social movement must claim and demon-

strate that the current institutions are failing to solve the problem. If this is done successfully, the need for change becomes evident and rallies people to the cause.

3. **Prepare for nonviolent grassroots action.** Jesus knew and demonstrated that lasting change comes through nonviolence. The Caesars are long gone, despite their control of the means of violence, repression, and wealth. The little religion Jesus founded is still here, thousands of years later, with well over a billion followers. It has changed the world. Martin Luther King Jr. believed in nonviolence as well, and his work is continued by his daughter at the King Center, Dr. Bernice King. The Civil Rights Movement is one of the most momentous movements in US history. Nonviolence is the only way to lasting change.

4. **Frame it.** Social movement scholars talk endlessly about frames, framing, and frame alignment. It means educating the public and enlisting their support, because enlisting more and more people toward change ultimately leads to change. How the issue is framed makes all the difference. Consider again the Civil Rights Movement. The problem they specified was racial segregation. The movement could have been framed as "you should join the movement because racial segregation is unfair." That would appeal to some people, but likely not most. Instead, the Civil Rights Movement's frame was "America is amazing. Let her live up to what she says she is—a land where everyone has the right to the pursuit of life, liberty, and happiness. Racial segregation prevents America from being fully America, from realizing the American Dream." See the difference. How a social movement is framed is the make-or-break moment of many movements. Let's return to the cause of reparations discussed in the previous chapter. Reparations will never occur just because they are right, good, or moral. There is too much vested interest by those who have benefitted from unjust systems. Thus, it will take a substantial social movement, and it must find the right frame—frame alignment—that resonates with a substantial swath of people. It doesn't seem a stretch that the reparations movement could find a successful frame in learning lessons from the Civil Rights Movement. "America, live up to your promise that all can pursue life, liberty, and happiness. No one should start out with a broken back in that pursuit, but that is where we find ourselves. We need reparations to finally let America be the shining city on a hill it has dreamed to be." Perhaps the move-

ment would be called the "Make It Right Campaign" or the "Dream the Dream Campaign."
5. **Acknowledge opposition**. Any movement will encounter resistance and opposition. A movement, therefore, must prepare for such opposition and have a plan to counter it. Failure to do so will mean movement failure. Study and time must be invested not only in identifying the opposition but also in understanding the reasons and tactics of the opposition.
6. **Dedicate to long-term goals**. Though at times it can feel as such, change never occurs overnight. It takes many years. In fact, most often, it takes decades of continuous work to lead to meso- or macro-level change. Those in movements must plan for the long game if they are truly dedicated to and want to realize change. Plenty of otherwise well-intentioned social movements flame out after a few years because they were not built with the long game in mind. Leaders of such movements need to be honest with themselves and their followers. Small changes may occur, but the ultimate goals will take several decades, so commit to such a time frame.
7. **Recognize success**. Because of the long time frame, any small success must be celebrated. Each step is both a movement toward the ultimate goal and the best fuel for catapulting the movement forward. Never let a success go uncelebrated.
8. **Retain success**. Successes are to be celebrated, but they also must be retained. They cannot be forgotten or allowed to dissipate. They must become the new starting point for the movement, so social movement leaders do well to clearly plan for how they will retain each success and use it to get ever closer to the ultimate goal.

Social movements are key to kingdom racial change. We have considered the eight essential components of successful social movements—that is, social movements that reach their goals. Social movements often start small, but they must grow in concentric rings. In the inner circle are the leaders and visionaries. The larger circle around the inner circle contains the first adopters of the vision, those who are highly committed and do much of the organizing work of the movement. And that work is to build a larger circle around them of supporters of the cause who advocate from their own social locations for the changes championed by the movement, perhaps speaking on social media or talking directly with friends and family. Their work is ultimately to help generate an ever-growing final circle of mass supporters for the cause of the movement. In our context, social movements, then, are about creating expanding social networks, coordinated through organizations, for the kingdom racial change.

Several models exist for growing a social movement. Rev. Ev. spent eighteen years of his life doing exactly this in the Chicago organization first run by Barack Obama called Developing Communities Project. They had a clear strategy for growth, complete with specific targets. For Rev. Ev., that included having at least twenty-five one-on-one meetings per month with community leaders, recruiting at least one pastor per week to the movement, and holding Action Meetings with at least 250 community members in attendance. In Action Meetings, church-based community members gather to create action plans for community improvement. The meetings also galvanize support for the larger movement. In short, if you are serious about kingdom racial change, the good news is that there are tried-and-true methods for recruiting, organizing, and, ultimately, changing society.

Conclusion

We make true and lasting kingdom racial change via the meso-level trinity of social networks, organizations, and social movements. At the church and Christian community levels, we advocate directly that the ROW must go. The Religion of Whiteness twists and contorts our Christian communities, leaving wounded people and organizations scattered along its path. The work for kingdom racial change at this level is to root out the ROW. We explored the main steps in doing so.

For large-scale change, such as reparations or changing our educational system to be more just, our tool is a social movement. We explored the eight characteristics of successful social movements. Sometimes, no such movements exist, and we may be part of starting one. But our default should always be to assume such a movement does exist, and we can look for how to get involved, be that individually, with our social network, or with our organizations.

Our building blocks for kingdom racial change enrich our understanding of the role of social networks, organizations, and social movements. Building Block 8 reads, "When God puts you in a position to help others of different racial groups thrive, do so." How does that happen?

The Meso-Level Change Levers

It occurs through our social networks, as we will not encounter those of different racial backgrounds but through our social networks. And what does it mean to be in a position to help? Most often, it means having the opportunity through our social networks and organizations to connect others to resources, be that jobs, finances, schooling, health care, counseling, or other benefits. In short, we realize this key building block of kingdom racial change through our meso-level belongings.

We have one more vital level to explore in our quest for kingdom racial change—the micro-level of us as individuals and our relationships with family and close friends. We do so in chapter 7, addressing our final building blocks.

7

Healthy Micro-Level Worlds and God's Love Offensive

Here is what we have learned thus far: We can and must make macro changes for kingdom racial change. We do so through the meso-level levers of social networks, organizations, and social movements. And, it turns out, we need to make changes at this meso level, too, for our organizations are far too often racialized and reflective of the very issues we must overcome for kingdom racial change.

But none of these changes succeed without a deeply healthy micro-level world, the intimate world of our relationships with family and friends, as well as our own personal lives. What exactly we mean by "deeply healthy" is the topic of this chapter. It is the final link in a three-tiered system that God has given us for realizing kingdom racial change.

Our Direction

To have deeply healthy micro-level worlds, let us consider Romans 12:2. The New International Version reads, "Do not conform to the pattern of this world, but be transformed by the renewing of your mind. Then you will be able to test and approve what God's will is—his good, pleasing, and perfect will." This powerful verse tells us to *transform* that which is *deformed* so we can *conform* to our God-given design. How are we to transform the deformed to conform to our God-given reality?

By renewing our minds. The false, incessant teachings of the world pollute our minds. We will explore some of those false teachings below. The only way to transform our minds is to wash away false and harmful understandings by *flooding our minds with new knowledge*. We must think and understand anew so we can then know the will of God.

As we flood our minds anew, here is a truth: We are not seeking God's will for our lives. Instead, we are seeking God's will for the world. God invites us to be part of God's work in the world, and we must decide to accept the invitation, reject it, or ignore it. Life's full blessings come as we take the steps of faith to follow God's calling to be part of the Almighty's work in the world. In so doing, we live into our purpose for being created, and we join the fellow saints who have their arms extended upward, holding to the garment of Jesus. For a deeper understanding of this teaching, we highly recommend the powerful book *Experiencing God: Knowing and Doing the Will of God*.[1]

Our point here is that our internal work as Christians is to renew our minds with the teachings of Christ, with deep friendships with fellow believers, and through confession and accountability to one another. In so doing, we come to hear God's voice and understand God's work in the world. As we do, God will call each of us to play a special role in the work of transforming the world. But there is an inflection point in this process. When we are called, we will experience a crisis of faith. This crisis is because the call will be bigger than what we can do on our own. It will be bigger than what we think we are skilled enough to do. At this very point, we find out if we truly have faith, for we either step out into the uncertainty of God's call or say no to it, choosing instead the certainty of our present reality. Let us pray for one another that we take the step of faith each time we are called.

Recall, for example, that Dr. David, while driving home and thinking of the wonderful things God was doing with the all-Black men's group, heard God tell him to extend the group beyond Black men. He knew full well the risks of doing so. He knew the pain that could be introduced, the risk of white men taking over, and the risk of the Black men leaving. He knew there would be resistance. But he stepped out in faith. He first reached out to Rev. Ev., who himself knew that, in earthly terms, such would be a bad decision, but who said he would follow God in this. They then reached out to the other men in the group, most of whom opposed expanding outside of their circle. Here was a true crisis point: if Dr. David truly heard God's call, then he must be obedient despite the risk.

---

1. Henry T. Blackaby and Claude V. King, *Experiencing God: Knowing and Doing the Will of God* (Nashville, TN: Lifeway Church Resources, 1990).

Part 2. Making Kingdom Racial Change

Both he and Rev. Ev., at the point of crisis, took the risky step of faith. The result has been something not even they could have envisioned. God can, and God will.

It All Starts with Me . . . Not

Here are common phrases we hear people say, both outside and inside the church:

> I've got to get my life right, then I can . . .
> I need to love myself to love others.
> I am in my head.
> I have worked hard to get where I am.
> You are bringing me down.
> You are robbing me of my joy.
> I can do it myself, thank you.
> I need "me time."
> We can only have quality relationships to the extent that we are each emotionally healthy.
> Being a Christian is first about my relationship with Christ, so that has to be my primary focus.
> I need to live my truth.
> Everyone needs to find and live into their own truth.
> You worry about yourself; I'll worry about me.
> At least I am not like that person. I am okay.
> Sure, I've got faults, but those people have more.
> I got to get mine.
> I am me: take it or leave it.
> I am what I am.
> You can be anything you want to be.
> I'm worth it.
> I did it my way.
> I want to find my person, the one who makes me whole.
> I love you; you make me feel so good, so complete.
> God helps those who help themselves.

In our call to renew our minds, it is thinking in these ways that deforms us. Christian or not, we may all struggle with such thinking. In fact, you may be struggling right now to see what is the problem with at least some of these ways of thinking. Isn't being a Christian about my relationship with Christ? And if so, shouldn't that be my primary focus? Am I wrong to want to find love with someone? Doesn't almost everyone want that, Christian or not?

We will unpack these, but if you are struggling at all with any of these ways of thinking needing to be altered, we are succeeding in making our point. It is easy to say we need to renew our minds to be consistent with Christ's. But what that means in actual practice is an ongoing struggle.

This leads us to critique the number-one focus of many of the above ways of thinking. They assume I, me, and myself do the deciding, do the work of renewing, and make the determinations. The false teaching here is that we are individual Christian islands, shaping and determining the outcomes of our lives. We are each the center of our own story. Such a set of lies dooms us to anxiety, depression, sadness, feeling like a failure, and endlessly struggling to be enough. This is not the Christian path whatsoever.

When we are called to be Christians, we join a continent of the faithful. Through our intimate relationships and our larger Christian community, we together engage in the process of renewing our minds. We do so primarily by engaging in discipleship, a process that, by definition, involves more than one person. So the first step in the renewing of our minds is to accept that we must be with others whether we are being discipled or doing the discipling.

A second incessant lie told to us as Americans is it is truly about me. We desperately want "it" to be about ourselves, and we are told repeatedly it is. In fact, we are oftentimes told it is harmful not to make it about us, as not "taking charge of our life" can lead us to be co-dependent or susceptible to authoritarian leaders. We want to be important, we want to be loved, we want attention, we want to matter. But in the renewing of our minds, a major key teaching of Christianity is that all of this is guaranteed and already settled. God so loved the world (every single one of us and our systems, organizations, etc.) that he gave his only begotten Son. By definition, without exception and not open for debate, we are loved, we matter, and we are of eternal importance. We don't achieve it, and we don't search for it; we don't take charge of it for ourselves. It is a given fact. One of our personal favorite sayings is that there is nothing we can do to make God love us more, and there is nothing we can do to make God love us less. To quote the title of singer Rachel Lampa's song, we are "perfectly loved." Our second step in renewing our minds is to let this truth flood over us, to accept it, and to proceed to live as if it is true, which, in fact, it is. We will need the support of our Christian friends and family and of our larger Christian community when we are tempted to waver from this truth.

Thus follows the third vital step in the renewing of our minds: accepting that we do not stand alone. We stand in community. We must seek out Christian friends, family, mentors, and eventually mentees. We are to support and encourage one another in the renewing of our minds. Iron sharpens iron, as the famous saying goes, and it is most certainly true in the Christian life.

As we are pursuing kingdom racial change, we see in the world's teachings the ongoing seeds of the problem. The world's teachings require both comparison and relativity. How do I know if I am okay? How do I know if I am good-looking, smart, or special? By comparing myself to others and deciding it is so. Sometimes I will determine I am indeed smart, based on my comparison. But other times, I will encounter people who I determine are smarter than me. When that happens, I will either feel bad about myself, questioning my worth, or I will come to dislike or discount those other persons so that I will not have to conclude they are actually smarter than me.

Such ways of worldly thinking invite, accept, and may even demand inequality, injustice, and endless, exhausting competition. Comparison is about ranking, hierarchy, and assessing value and worth relative to others. The fourth step as we seek to be renewed in Christ's likeness is to flood our minds with the Christian truth that comparison, ranking, hierarchy, and assigning differential value to people is all to be left behind, swept into a dustbin of falsehoods. Instead, we train ourselves, with the support of other Christians, to think completely differently. Each of us has different skills, gifts, experiences, social networks, and more, but we all are valued equally in the kingdom. God has assigned us different roles, using our different gifts in different places and times to do God's work on earth collectively. We dare not rank God's assignments. We have no basis by which to make such a determination (compared to what?), and there is no gain to doing so. Recall Jesus's teaching that to whom much is given, much is expected (see Luke 12:48). I may say I have done twice as much as you in building God's kingdom, but if God expected me to do three times more because of the gifts given, in a ranking system, I would come up the "loser."

But it doesn't work this way in Christendom. Each of us stands together equally in need of Christ, equally reaching upward to touch the garment of Christ, equally empowered by the Holy Spirit to do the work we have been assigned. Our calling is to support one another in our collective work using our unique giftings and placement in the world.

In chapter 2, we arrived at a building block for kingdom racial change: Every single one of us occupies *a social location*—a specific place in the social world within a specific society within a specific historical moment (Building Block 2). We thus assess the world and suggest how it should be improved from our social location, what we know to be true. This fact is both positive and negative. The positive is that we have an important and unique view of the world. We can see and know in ways others cannot by virtue of where we stand. The negative is twofold: First, we too often conclude our view is either the only view or the best view. Second, our understandings are, on our own, parochial and limited to but a portion of the truth.

As we renew our minds, this building block becomes nothing but positive. We realize God has blessed us with a vital view of the world. And we humbly realize, completely, that we need others precisely because our unique view of the world necessarily limits us. The beauty is that in this realization we find the blessing and joy of the diverse Christian community as God calls believers from all social locations. Part of our calling and our joy is harnessing our diversity for God's huge work in the world. It is messy, to be sure, but it is at the same time wondrous and powerful, as it is something God does as we allow our minds to be renewed.

A Deeply Healthy Micro-Level World Knows What Love Is

Jesus tells us: "If you love me, keep my commands" (John 14:15). Who is this Jesus that he should give commands? We are the masters of our own fate. We decide what is best for us. No one tells us what to do. Well, unless we say we love Jesus. Then Jesus tells us what to do. We bow before our Lord as we renew our minds.

But in addition to "keep my commands," there is a second part to Jesus's words: "If you love me." *What does love mean to Jesus?* People who speak languages other than English often marvel at English speakers' frequent and wide-ranging use of the word *love*. We love God, we love our spouse, we love our children, we love our pet, we love chocolate, we love rainy or sunny days, we love that song, we love the smell of roses, we love our job, we love our classes, we love how someone makes us feel, we love our friends, we love steak and eggs, we love bean sprouts, we love social media, we love a particular airline, and on it goes. Clearly, love cannot mean love in the same way across all of these contexts.

The problem is twofold. First, in English we only have one word for the different types of love. So, we end up using it as if our appreciation of a song is of the same order as our love of God. Second, we don't know what we mean by love. In our culture, love is our choice and a feeling. We fall in and out of it. But it is never defined, partly because it has somehow been decided that we each get to determine on our own what love is and what we love.

As new Christians (or even if we are raised in a Christian home), we often continue relying on a cultural understanding of love, confused for English speakers by the lack of diversity of terms for different types of love. Perhaps the best we do is hear a teaching on the Bible's love chapter, 1 Corinthians 13. We might even go so far as to recall that love is patient and love is kind. Beyond that, we don't remember much, and certainly, this understanding does little to shift the cultural definition of love we have been given and unconsciously adopted.

Fortunately, we don't have to guess what Jesus meant by love. He told us directly:

"Whoever has my commands and keeps them is the one who loves me. The one who loves me will be loved by my Father, and I too will love them and manifest myself to them." (John 14:21)

"Anyone who loves me will obey my teaching." (John 14:23)

"Anyone who does not love me will not obey my teaching." (John 14:24)

"A new command I give you: Love one another. As I have loved you, so you must love one another." (John 13:34)

Healthy Micro-Level Worlds and God's Love Offensive

"My command is this: Love each other as I have loved you. Greater love has no one than this: to lay down one's life for one's friends. You are my friends if you do what I command." (John 15:12–14)

The very definition of love taught to us directly from our Lord is that love means obedience to his commands and that the greatest form of love is the one Jesus himself demonstrated, to lay down one's life for another. In short, love is *obedience to Christ's teachings and sacrifice for others*. Such a definition is light-years away from the larger culture's teachings of love. It is not an emotion, though it can involve emotions. It is not self-determined. It is not relative. It is not me-centered. It is not a negotiation.

Dietrich Bonhoeffer, among others, has provided us with wonderful insight into the contrast of what he calls human love versus spiritual love—in other words, the love Jesus is talking about:

> Human love is directed to the other person for his own sake, spiritual love loves him for Christ's sake.

> Human love has little regard for truth. It makes the truth relative, since nothing, not even the truth, must come between it and the beloved person.

> Human love makes itself an end in itself.

> Spiritual love . . . comes from Jesus Christ, it serves him alone.

> What love is, only Christ tells in his Word. Contrary to all my own opinions and convictions, Jesus Christ will tell me what love toward the brethren really is.

> Spiritual love does not desire but rather serves.[2]

If love is serving others and obeying Christ's commands, we would all benefit internally by diving into a deep study of Christ's commands. We cannot do that in great detail here, but we encourage you to do so

---

2. Bonhoeffer, *Life Together*, 34–35.

Part 2. Making Kingdom Racial Change

by finding Christian books on the topic. For our purposes, however, we offer twelve such commands and teachings (one for each disciple):

1. "But I tell you, love your enemies and pray for those who persecute you" (Matt. 5:44).
2. "This, then, is how you should pray: 'Our Father in heaven, hallowed be your name, your kingdom come, your will be done, on earth as it is in heaven'" (Matt. 6:9–11).
3. "Therefore I tell you, do not worry about your life, what you will eat or drink; or about your body, what you will wear. Is not life more than food, and the body more than clothes?" (Matt. 6:25).
4. "So in everything, do to others what you would have them do to you, for this sums up the Law and the Prophets" (Matt. 7:12).
5. "As you go, proclaim this message: 'The kingdom of heaven has come near.' Heal the sick, raise the dead, cleanse those who have leprosy, drive out demons. Freely you have received; freely give" (Matt. 10:7–8).
6. "Every kingdom divided against itself will be ruined, and every city or household divided against itself will not stand" (Matt. 12:25).
7. "Then Jesus said to his disciples, 'Whoever wants to be my disciple must deny themselves and take up their cross and follow me. For whoever wants to save their life will lose it, but whoever loses their life for me will find it'" (Matt. 16:24–25; see also Mark 8:34–35 and Luke 9:23–24).
8. "Therefore, whoever takes the lowly position of this child is the greatest in the kingdom of heaven" (Matt. 18:4).
9. "Anyone who wants to be first must be the very last, and the servant of all" (Mark 9:35).
10. "Now that I, your Lord and Teacher, have washed your feet, you also should wash one another's feet" (John 13:14).
11. "I am the way and the truth and the life. No one comes to the Father except through me" (John 14:6).
12. "I am the vine; you are the branches. If you remain in me and I in you, you will bear much fruit; apart from me you can do nothing" (John 15:5).

Consider the themes of these commands and teachings. Jesus talks an incredible amount about the *kingdom of God*—what it is, parables to illustrate it, why it is so important, that we should seek it, that it will come, and that we must pray for it. He also talks about his role in the cosmic story—he is our peace, he is our salvation, he is the way, he is truth, he is life. The focus is on the kingdom and Christ. We are beneficiaries. We are not the story itself.

Our role in the story is to stay focused on Christ. Each of us has our hand extended upward, all touching the garment of Christ. This is our singular unity. This is our common link. There is no earthly commonality, only the Christ we have all been called to. We are to love others, including our enemies. And we indeed will have enemies who persecute us, even fellow Christians. But we are not to worry, we are not to be afraid. We are to minister, proclaim, and work for the kingdom on earth as it is in heaven. We can only do such things by each keeping our arms extended upward, touching Christ's garment both for our unity and his leading.

Why should we focus in such detail on love and Christ's commands? Because true kingdom racial change can only occur when God's people put away their earthly desires and ambitions and instead focus on loving Jesus by obeying his commands. We must stay focused on our only unifying reality. We must stay dependent on our only commonality. And we must understand how to truly love. When we do so, we will not need to be convinced we need kingdom racial change. We will pray for it, we will beg for it, we will weep for it, we will sacrifice for it. We will do so for one and only one reason—because Christ, through the Holy Spirit, will indwell and empower us.

No more will we say, "Stick to the gospel instead of talking about race." No more will we want to ignore injustice. No more will we wish to blame others for inequalities and suffering. A Christian community is a people intertwined with one another. It is a body with many parts, each of which must be supported and tended to for the body to function as it is designed.

Our Building Blocks

God gives all people and cultures unique attributes that, when used properly, lead to God's glory. Our three remaining building blocks for this micro-level chapter are intertwined with the social-location building block we have already discussed. Recall that our social location—our place in the world at the current time in history—gives us a unique and needed perspective. As we mature in Christ, we realize that this perspective is both exceptional and but a portion of God's reality. So, we earnestly seek out others as we desire to know God and God's creation.

This is why our Building Block 9, the need for cross-racial relationships, is essential for racial change. We will not, on our own or with others highly similar to us, be transformative of meso- and macro-level realities that must be altered for racial justice and righteousness to occur. We must work with one another in deep relationships. In fact, the cognitive scientists Steven Sloman and Philip Fernbach, in their book *The Knowledge Illusion: Why We Never Think Alone,* argue that humans have hive minds, meaning we only think well through cooperation and community.[3] Even to think, they find, we must do so in the context of others. This is how God has intentionally created us.

Yet our building block of cross-racial relationships does not stop at simply making friends. We learned in chapter 4 that we must have key characteristics in place for such relationships to be effective. Such relationships must strive for cooperation as they reach toward shared goals. This is the wonder of Christians seeking kingdom racial change—we have the shared goal built in, and we can only achieve it through coordinated cooperation.

Such relationships also need the support of an external authority, such as a pastor, boss, or even senior family members. Vitally important, too, is that those involved in such relationships will have to meet as equals. In our worldly eyes, differences such as being of diverse social classes or professions, being employed or not employed, being married or not, differences in how we speak, and other such factors mean we do not meet as equals. In each case, there is an implied ranking system. The higher-ranked person will eventually "take charge" or have things done their way rather than working cooperatively toward a shared solution and toward a shared goal. As we have seen with the Men's Unity Group, when the original white leaders did not like the direction of the group, they declared what would and what would not be talked about and eventually left the group, taking their resources with them.

Allowing such ranking systems to shape Christian relationships cannot be our reality. When we understand what it means to be Christian, we understand we are all equal before Christ. And that is the gift God gives us for creating powerful cross-racial relationships in which

---

3. Steven Sloman and Philip Fernbach, *The Knowledge Illusion: Why We Never Think Alone* (New York: Riverhead Books, 2018).

we meet as equals, allowing us to undertake the work of God together. Part of doing this is to stress that all cultures have advantages and all cultures have negatives. We provide counterweights for one another. Thus, our Building Block 3 is that there are Black (and Native American, Hispanic, Asian, Middle Eastern, etc.) advantages. We specifically noted in chapter 2 some of the Black advantages over white culture—more religious, more faith, greater reliance on and closeness to God, more close friends, more kin, and a higher percentage in Christian mentoring relationships. Again, all groups have advantages and uniqueness they bring to relationships and organizations. This is yet another of God's blessings. We make change at the larger levels only insofar as we have strong micro-level cross-racial relationships where we truly view one another as equals, each able to teach and learn from the other equally.

The distorting power of the fallen world leads us to our Building Block 5: creating healthy environments in which to grow up. Perhaps nothing else is as important. The devil works to disrupt us at our genesis and maturation periods, attempting to deform us for life. We, therefore, must counter this attack on our children with our own offensive. We must focus intense attention on creating social environments that maximize stability, security, and faith development.

Poverty, crime, sickness, divorce, and abuse all generate social environments that damage our children. It is true that we can find examples of those who are able to overcome such limitations—two of the authors of this book are indeed examples. But the "success" rate for people who grow up in such contexts and come out with minimal scarring is painfully and unacceptably low.

In our prayers, in our work together in our cross-racial relationships, in our churches, and wherever it is possible, we must seek to create healthy environments for our children, no matter where they live, what their parents do, or their color. Let us strive to give every child a true chance at dignity and true opportunity. We don't want a world where Rev. Ev. grows up having to move countless times due to evictions, job loss by his parents, and unsafety. We don't want a world where Rev. Ev. is hounded by gang members or constantly suspected by law enforcement to be doing something wrong because of his color and location. We don't want a world where Rev. Ev. has to leave college and is never able to return because the immediate need to make money to help the family is so urgent and intense that a college degree must be left behind. We don't want a world where Dr. David and his siblings grow up in an environment so full of toxins that they are guaranteed to suffer physical calamities. We don't want a world where Dr. David must spend hours waiting on and riding buses simply to get some basic groceries. We don't want a world where Dr. David has to fight, scratch, and claw to get an education while being told at every turn he is not good enough, not bright enough, not motivated enough, and, in short, just not enough. We also don't want a world where Emerson is told other groups are not as good as he is. We don't want a world where he is given a false, distorted sense of reality. And we don't want a world where he is separated from other Christians due to the world's lies, sinful structures and social arrangements, and wrong teachings.

We want all of our children to have a chance. We want them to have healthy environments, and so we seek to create them within the spheres of influence God has given, not only us, but also to our friends, our social networks, our churches, and other organizations, and ultimately, through the wise use of social movements.

But how can we tackle such a huge issue? The US Centers for Disease Control and Prevention (CDC) is charged with thinking about such issues. They outline the trilogy needed for children to have healthy environments:[4]

1. **Safety**: Children must be able to grow up in environments where they are free from fear of violence or harm, be that physical or emotional.
2. **Stability**: Children need predictability and consistency in their lives, from minimal neighborhood moves to set bedtimes to not having to experience caregivers who oscillate in temperament.
3. **Nurturing**: Humans have few instincts. We only survive and mature insofar as we are cared for and taught by others. Children need to know they are loved, they need boundaries, they need the freedom to explore within those boundaries, they need proper food and exercise, and they need to be discipled in the love and ways of Christ (as you can imagine, this last clause the CDC does not say, but we know it is essential).

These three characteristics can guide anything we do to create healthy environments for children. We seek to provide our children

---

4. Centers for Disease Control, *Essentials for Childhood*, n.d., accessed June 3, 2024, at https://tinyurl.com/4xsc2rte.

with safety, stability, and nurture. We start, of course, with our own children and grandchildren. We sacrifice for them (love is sacrifice) so they may have maximal opportunity to grow up healthy and be loving people themselves. Yet, our guess is that almost anyone reading this book who has children or grandchildren already does this.

The issue is, of course, that far too many children do not experience such environments. For example, according to the National Institutes of Health, about one out of every four American children will experience abuse (physical, sexual, emotional) or severe neglect during their childhood. At least one out of every six children in the United States—according to the US Census Bureau—grows up in poverty, ensuring a lack of many needed resources. And stunningly, over one-quarter of all African American children in the United States live in rental households threatened with eviction each year, and over 12 percent are indeed evicted *each year*.[5] The experience that Rev. Ev. and his siblings had more than once growing up is a shamefully common occurrence.

So here is what we can do. Let us think again at the three levels of social life. Consider all the children you encounter at the micro level through your daily living and through your family and friends. Consciously ask yourself, alone or within your family and friend groups, "Do any children I know seem to lack the trilogy of provisions?" If yes, act. How you act matters, and it will depend on the situation. If you suspect abuse of any type, report it to the proper authorities. If you see a need—such as a lack of food—seek assistance from agencies that exist for such needs, or consider helping directly if the child's caregivers are agreeable and you and your family or friend groups are able.

If we do this, we will see significant improvements for significant numbers of children. But we have two more levels from which to achieve kingdom racial change for children. At the meso level of our churches and our social networks, we can be part of supporting organizations that already exist to create supportive environments for children. We can do so through volunteering, giving resources, and even, for some of us, making it our career. When we need to advocate for significant changes in laws, policies, and practices, we can join or support social movements designed to do exactly that. Let's consider just one example. We have seen many a church "adopt" a school to provide support for

---

5. See Julie Craven, "Eviction Is One of the Biggest Health Risks Facing Black Children," New America, December 7, 2023, https://tinyurl.com/4vm4v2k9.

the children who attend that school. The Men's Unity Group, in fact, has joined Dr. David's church's adoption of a grade school on Chicago's south side. They have participated in praying for everyone at the school, visiting the school, and attempting to meet needs as they arise.

Even when we are fully addressing the issue at the micro and meso levels, we will fight a never-ending battle unless we realize macro-change as well. Helping individual children or individual schools isn't enough if children are growing up in high-poverty-concentrated neighborhoods, high-crime neighborhoods, neighborhoods with environmental toxins, or neighborhoods with high divorce, high unemployment, high eviction, or high imprisonment. Want to make a change at this level? We suggest returning to chapter 5 for three recommended routes. Or you can identify another route—such as seeking change in eviction policies or environmental regulation.

The important points for us all to remember are these. First, we never, ever make change on our own. We are not designed to do so. Second, as we work with others, we never, ever realize kingdom racial change all at once. We make incremental changes. So third, we must never be overwhelmed by the vastness of the problem. God is coordinating a love offensive across our land. Our call is to play our role, to hear where we are being called, and to follow that call. So, fourth and finally, we seek to make change by focusing on one macro issue only. If we are passionate about seeing kingdom racial change realized, this is a difficult precept to hold to. We will want to do more. Don't fall into that trap. We must put our faith on the line and trust that, just as God calls us to a particular area of change, God's call for other areas of change is going out to other Christians.

Conclusion

The intimate micro-level world of our spiritual development and our close friendships and family ties needs to be healthy and mature if we are to see kingdom racial change. This chapter has explored that we make this so through the renewing of our minds, through changing to other-centered concern, through understanding what Jesus taught us is love, and through following Jesus's commands. We then turned to considering and applying our micro-level building blocks of social location, cross-racial friendships, understanding and using the reality that all cultures and peoples bring unique advantages to the table, and creating healthy environments for children.

We focused especially on creating healthy environments for children. One of Emerson's adult sons is a forester for the state of Minnesota. His job is to raise vast forests of healthy trees, which will be logged, and then start the process over again. In his job, he knows the single most important role in creating healthy forests is at the point when seedlings are planted into the ground. They must be planted correctly, they must receive the proper nutrients, and they must be protected from predators and disease. To do so, he keeps a detailed eye on the young seedlings for the first several years, providing them with special care.

It works in the very same way with humans. To have a nation and world that realizes kingdom racial change, we acknowledge that the single most important path is to give children healthy environments in which to grow. Even more than trees, humans must be raised in safe, stable, and nurturing environments. If we allow the destruction that currently impacts our children—so deeply unequally by race—to continue, the battle is over before it begins. In God's love offensive, his seedlings receive special and constant attention.

We end this chapter with an unfortunate reality that we must consider. A massive difference exists between knowing how to work for change and actually doing it. The "actually doing it" takes motivation, time, energy, resources, and cooperation. We can mean well, but it all too often gets lost in doing life. We struggle in school or work, we have a bad relationship or a breakdown of a relationship, we get ill, we go through depression, or there is no money. These reasons and many others mean even if we know the exact three-step plan for kingdom racial change, it doesn't happen.

This is the devil's work: keep us preoccupied, get our attention somewhere else, put up roadblocks. So, know this: if you are committed to kingdom racial change, roadblocks are guaranteed, and the more committed you are to kingdom racial change, the more roadblocks you will encounter. We have found that two complications, in particular, will rear their ugly heads if you are truly moving toward God-desired racial change: (1) people's egos get in the way, and (2) relational difficulties get people to simply quit. These two roadblocks, then, are killers of kingdom racial change. So far, the devil has won endless victories with these two repeating roadblocks. We would be wise, then, to consider each in turn. When you encounter these roadblocks, return to this portion of the book.

Part 2. Making Kingdom Racial Change

Even as we renew our minds, we all have egos. Even the gentlest, most caring people ultimately have their own opinions, preferences, and desires. At some point in working for change, somebody (and usually more than just one person) will lose sight of the goal and focus instead on their own status or getting their way. It will become about them rather than the change itself. We have seen this pattern over and over. People want change, but they will want recognition for their sacrifice. They will want to direct the decision-making. They will need to feel important. As Dietrich Bonhoeffer so well put it:

> But the important thing is that a Christian community should know that somewhere in it there will certainly be 'a reasoning among them, which of them should be the greatest.' It is the struggle of the natural man for self-justification. He finds it only in comparing himself with others, in condemning and judging others. Self-justification and judging others go together, as justification by grace and serving others go together.[6]

This then leads to the second change killer: broken relationships. Power struggles ensue, people begin playing politics, emotionally unhealthy people become even more unhealthy, and the end result is at least someone (again, usually more than one person) leaves the organization or group, unable to work and serve in what they perceive as an unhealthy and even toxic environment. These are the change killers that you can expect.

What can be done? As you embark on working for change, guard your own heart first. Never stop renewing your mind in partnership with others. Plead with God to keep you from becoming the person whose ego gets in the way. And beseech God to protect the relationships you have and the ones you will develop. Begin every day with these petitions.

Second, if you consider becoming part of an already-existing organization for change, invest in due diligence. What has been the track record of the organization? Who is leading it, and what has been people's experience working for this leader? What is the turnover rate in the organization? And, ultimately, what has the organization accomplished? Does the organization have clear goals, and has it progressed on them?

---

6. Bonhoeffer, *Life Together*, 91.

Healthy Micro-Level Worlds and God's Love Offensive

Third, and finally, if you do encounter ego and relationships turning sour, have a plan for how to handle this. The wrong plan is simply to quit. God commands us to work for his righteous kingdom. We don't stop doing that because of roadblocks and bad eggs. These realities are part of the landmines the devil will always place in our way to convince us to give up. Rather, we work our way around the landmines. This may mean we have to leave an organization for another one working for change. It may mean working to repair a relationship. It may even mean sticking it out even in the face of the issues because the larger goal is being reached despite the ego(s) and difficult relationships. God will let you know the path if you ask, but never give up and never let fallen people and broken relationships lead you off the path of working for kingdom racial change.

Each of us authors has experienced multiple rounds of these roadblocks. Sometimes we are the problem—we lost our way. Sometimes others are the problem. Sometimes we are all the problem. Sometimes we cannot tell where the problem stems from. The temptation each time is to give up and walk away. We are eternally grateful that God has kept us on the path toward kingdom racial change, despite major detours and roadblocks. Our failures do not define us. Christ defines us, and Christ defines all of our Christian siblings. We stumble, we fall, but we get back up, knowing we are not in and of ourselves worthy to continue. But we also know that Christ is worthy (Revelation 5 tells us that the living creatures and the elders sing he is worthy!). And that is what matters, not our worthiness.

While in graduate school working for his doctorate, Emerson received advice from a more advanced graduate student. She said that doctoral degrees don't go to the smartest people; they go to those who don't give up. Kingdom racial change doesn't come because we are smart or worthy or special; it comes because we won't stop working for a better day, by being laser-focused on our call and by knowing that it is Christ's worthiness that propels us forward.

To that, we say, Amen and glory to God.

Postlude

Not long before writing this postlude, my wife and I (Dr. David) visited Thailand. My younger son joined us during our stay in Phuket. My wife and I immediately became keenly aware that we were treated differently in Thailand than in our daily experience in the United States. The kindness directed toward us was hard to fathom. For example, during the breakfast buffet the waitress and manager catered to us with such kind attention that we thought perhaps they were mistaking us for foreign royalty. They even took a picture of us on our last day in Phuket. Even though we saw few people who looked like us in Thailand, we were treated with dignity and respect. There were no condescending stares or looks of fear or suspicion, or the "What are they doing here?" looks we receive on a regular basis at home. We were enthusiastically greeted wherever we went. And it wasn't just us. We noticed that many Thais were listening to Black music. They seemed to be enamored with American Black culture.

What our family was experiencing in Thailand was the absence of racism toward Black Americans. We have to admit we did not think such a thing was possible, but what a vision of what could be. If only we had this way of life back home! The feeling of freedom and empowerment that we experienced in Thailand was exhilarating, like breathing in the clear, fresh air for the first time. With our lungs full, our spirits were energized. It was the direct result of the absence of racism toward Black Americans.

I realized that the freedom and empowerment I experienced in Thailand, if it were even approached in the United States, would produce an environment of confidence, which in turn would serve as a petri dish to incubate leaders of color. For example, our men's group has a leadership team consisting of two Black men, two white men, and one Asian man. Although we have a leadership team, Rev. Ev. and I, the two Black men, are the leaders and cofounders. Because of the diminished racism in our leadership group, it is far easier to lead, despite occasional challenges.

Given the racial context of the United States and in the church here, I believe it is necessary for people of color to lead multiracial groups for maximum effectiveness and care. Without the eyes of people of color, a multiracial group will lack appropriate direction. Thus, we must develop leaders of color to change the current path of the church—a path that is on a downward spiral. Our leadership team has had some disagreements, such as a hesitancy to move forward with a certain agenda that calls the white church out as the problem. But overall, our white and Asian brothers have agreed to tackle difficult topics of racism in the church.

I must admit that, in the process, we have spiritually evolved into a social movement to combat racism in the church and to separate the Religion of Whiteness from Christianity. As our relationships have strengthened over the years, so has our understanding of each other's cultures, especially our white and Asian team members understanding Black culture. The reason is that Michael and I are some of the only Black people they know or encounter on a regular basis. In fact, I was the first Black person our Asian team member has ever known, and that was at the age of his retirement. During his working life, he never knew Black people. Thus, the importance of constant engagement with our brothers during conferences, baseball games, small groups, and pulpit exchanges is invaluable. In so doing, we create friendships, we develop social networks, we support each other, we learn from each other, we challenge each other, we draw on the building blocks identified in this book, we seek to draw churches together, and we work for macro-level change. We also come to see the value of people of color in leadership, turning on its head the typical pattern seen throughout United States history. My goal is to place more people of color at the leadership table. That, indeed, will be a lynchpin and a sign of kingdom racial change.

Making Change

God's church is *inclusive*—every single person, every family, and every community is invited to come as they are into the community of Christ.

Postlude

God's church is also *exclusive*—of sin, harm to others, injustice, and ignoring the *imago dei* (image of God) within people and communities. Finally, and importantly, God's church is *intrusive*—we are not to stay as we are but to transform that which is deformed to conform to God's perfect design. We do so through the renewing of our minds, the renewing of friendships, the renewing of our churches, and the renewing of our society.

How do we do so? We have explored the three levels of life and outlined key changes needed at each level. These levels are intertwined. Because macro-level change is absolutely essential given the dramatic devastation the current arrangements and systems cause, we started first by recommending three possible macro-level changes and how to go about them. A significant part of the "how" is through meso-level levers, explored in chapter 6. Finally, these changes ultimately need healthy micro-level worlds, which we focused on in chapter 7.

A key purpose of this book is not to have readers overwhelmed but rather to encourage, focus, and provide a road map for making real change. A wise person once shared with us a simple rubric by which to think about making kingdom racial change, which we call *3D*: Discover, Develop, and Deploy.

> **Discover**: As you, your small group, your church, or other collective decide what specific change you are called to make, begin by discovering, which is exactly what you are doing in reading this book. The discover phase involves knowing the reality of the issue—such as the criminal-justice system—knowing why it occurs (reading about it, watching videos, talking to experts), and considering how the issue is impacted and intertwined with the three levels of social life. We are encouraged that you can find a tremendous and growing body of Christian literature on specific topics for making kingdom racial change.[1] Vitally essential, the discover phase involves going into serious prayer, asking for guidance, direction, and protection.
>
> **Develop**: The goal of the develop phase is to develop a strategic plan for change. You can certainly read about creating an effective strategic

---

1. We provide here a partial list, providing the authors' last names. The full citations can be found in the bibliography: Charles and Rah, Clemons and Stevens, Edmondson and Brennan, Edwards, Gilliard, Gray, Kwon and Thompson, Layton, Loritts, McKnight and Barringer, McNeil, Mingo and Jackson, Perkins, Romero, Rowe, Sanchez, Sanders, Swanson, Tisby, Twiss, and Woodley.

plan, but we note here that all strategic plans have five main components: (1) a *defined vision* of what success looks like, (2) an *assessment* of the current reality, (3) naming the *priorities and objectives* for achieving change, (4) defining who is *responsible* for realizing the objectives and by when, and (5) an *evaluation plan* to assess if success is being achieved. It is both exciting and essential to have a strategic plan for making effective change.

Deploy: Enact your strategic plan using the lessons from successful social movements. As we outlined in chapter 6, successful social movements deploy their strategic plan by making sure they have clearly identified the problem and the solution, showing institutional failures, preparing to make change nonviolently, educating others through framing the issue appropriately, making sure to assess who will oppose the change and how to address that opposition, dedicating themselves to long-term goals, recognizing successes whenever they are experienced, and then building upon those successes for further success.

Making kingdom racial change is accepting the call to be part of a massive movement that God is orchestrating. We accept that we are an instrument, but also that we are just one instrument, and our job is to play our instrument as best as possible. As a church or small group, select one and only one macro-level (or meso-level) item for change. For example, because educational inequality along racial lines is so detrimental to our society, and because we know smaller class sizes benefit all students but disproportionately those needing it most, you might advocate for smaller class sizes in your school district. This is entirely doable. Use *3D* to accomplish it. First, learn all that you can about the issue. This learning includes exploring whether there is an existing organization or collective advocating for this change already. If so, consider joining it. If not, start one. Second, develop by creating a strategic plan, or if you are joining an already-existing organization, by understanding its strategic plan and what your role will be within it. Finally, deploy. Engage in the appropriate coordinated actions to make real change. In this case, change means smaller class sizes and, thus, more teacher time for student learning.

Postlude

A Final Word

As illustrated so vividly throughout the Bible, and especially in books such as Daniel, Ezekiel, and Revelation, we are part of a cosmic battle with two sides: one led by Satan (the ancient serpent, the devil, Lucifer, the fiery red dragon, the accuser) and one led by God (the Almighty, the Holy One, Wonderful Conqueror, the Morning Star, the Alpha and Omega). Satan, having been cast down from heaven and having failed to destroy the child who is the Christ, now wages war on all "who keep God's commands and hold fast their testimony about Jesus" (Rev. 12:17).

Racial inequality, injustice, racism, division, and disunity are all the intended outcomes of Satan, who seeks to destroy humanity. As Christians, we are called to join God in this cosmic battle by pushing back against the evil twisting of God's design for humanity. Our call is not a part-time job. It is a lifetime of service that will indeed be filled with setbacks, confusion, and some lost battles. But we fear not. We know the final outcome. It is called victory. Kingdom racial change will occur, and we have the incredible opportunity to be part of this exhilarating cosmic call. May we hear, "Well done, my faithful servants!"

Building Blocks of Kingdom Racial Change

1. The mighty arm of racial power is that it is systemic.
2. Every single one of us occupies *a social location*—a specific place in the social world within a specific society within a specific historical moment.
3. We must understand Black advantages just as much as white advantages.
4. We have an urgent and essential need to root out the Religion of Whiteness from religious communities.
5. We must work to create healthy environments starting in childhood.
6. We must overcome the unholy link between race and class.
7. We, as Christians, have an amazing opportunity to change the structure of networks and connections.
8. When God puts us in a position to help others of different racial groups thrive, we must do so.
9. Cross-racial relationships are essential for kingdom racial change.
10. We must directly address whatever creates inequality between God's people.
11. Significant change often occurs through social movements, which occur through community organization and group cooperation.

Bibliography

Allport, Gordon. *The Nature of Prejudice*. Boston: Addison-Wesley, 1954.
Blackaby, Henry T., and Claude V. King. *Experiencing God: Knowing and Doing the Will of God*. Nashville: Lifeway Church Resources, 1990.
Block, Peter. *Community: The Structure of Belonging*. Oakland, CA: Berrett-Koehler, 2018.
Bonhoeffer, Dietrich. *Life Together: A Discussion of Christian Fellowship*. Translated by John W. Doberstein. San Francisco: HarperSanFrancisco, 1954.
Centers for Disease Control. *Essentials for Childhood*, n.d. Accessed June 3, 2024, at https://tinyurl.com/4xsc2rte.
Charles, Mark, and Soong-Chan Rah. *Unsettling Truths: The Ongoing Dehumanizing Legacy of the Doctrine of Discovery*. Downers Grove, IL: InterVarsity Press, 2019.
Cigarroa Kennedy, Camila, and Kori Stroub. "Recommendations Based on Results from the 2021–22 HISD Student Needs Survey." Houston Education Research Consortium, Kinder Institute for Urban Research, Rice University, November 2022. https://tinyurl.com/mtur2j6d.
Clemons, Josh, and Hazen Stevens. *Know, Own, Change: Journeying toward God's Heart for Reconciliation*. Chicago: Moody, 2022.
Craven, Julie. "Eviction Is One of the Biggest Health Risks Facing Black Children." *New America*, December 7, 2023. https://tinyurl.com/4vm4v2k9.
Darity, William, and A. Kirsten Mullen. *From Here to Equality: Reparations for Black Americans in the Twenty-First Century*. 2nd ed. Chapel Hill: University of North Carolina Press, 2022.
Edmondson, Christina, and Chad Brennan. *Faithful Antiracism: Moving Past Talk to Systemic Change*. Downers Grove, IL: InterVarsity Press, 2022.

Bibliography

Edwards, Dennis R. *Might from the Margins: The Gospel's Power to Turn the Tables on Injustice*. Harrisonburg, VA: Herald Press, 2020.

Edwards, Korie Little. *The Elusive Dream: The Power of Race in Interracial Churches*, updated version. New York: Oxford University Press, 2021.

Emerson, Michael O. "Residential Segregation Rewards Whites While Punishing People of Color." Kinder Institute for Urban Research, Rice University, September 21, 2020. https://tinyurl.com/3arctv5h.

Emerson, Michael O., and Glenn E. Bracey II. *The Religion of Whiteness: How Racism Distorts Christian Faith*. New York: Oxford University Press, 2024.

Gilliard, Dominique Dubois. *Rethinking Incarceration: Advocating for Restorative Justice*. Downers Grove, IL: InterVarsity Press, 2018.

———. *Subversive Witness: Scripture's Call to Leverage Privilege*. Grand Rapids: Zondervan, 2021.

Goza, Joel. *Rebirth of a Nation: Reparations and Remaking America*. Grand Rapids: Eerdmans, 2024.

Gray, Derwin L. *How to Heal Our Racial Divide*. Carol Stream, IL: Tyndale Momentum, 2022.

Howell, Junia. Eruka, 2024. https://www.eruka.org/.

———. "Eruka: Building a Just Economy." YouTube, 2024. https://tinyurl.com/mvkz4bnp.

Howell, Junia, and Elizabeth Korver-Glenn. "The Increasing Effect of Neighborhood Racial Housing Composition on Housing Values." *Social Problems* 68, no. 4 (2020): 1051–71.

———. "Neighborhood Racial Biases in 21st Century Housing Appraisals." Kinder Institute for Urban Research, Rice University, Working Paper, November 11, 2015.

Kaiser-Schatzlein, Robin. "This Is How America's Richest Families Stay That Way." *New York Times*, September 24, 2021.

Kinder Institute for Urban Research. Houston Education Research Consortium, 2024. https://tinyurl.com/yc32y543.

Korver-Glenn, Elizabeth. *Race Brokers: Housing Markets and Segregation in 21st Century Urban America*. New York: Oxford University Press, 2021.

Krysan, Maria, and Kyle Crowder. *Cycle of Segregation: Social Processes and Residential Stratification*. New York: Russell Sage Foundation, 2017.

Kwon, Duke L., and Gregory Thompson. *Reparations: A Christian Call for Repentance*. Grand Rapids: Brazos, 2021.

Layton, Aaron. *Dear White Christian*. Lawrenceville, GA: PCA Committee on Discipleship Ministries, 2017.

Bibliography

Lesueur, Beverly Anne. *Altgeld Gardens: Evolution of Culture and Education in an Isolated African American Community*. Dissertation, Loyola University Chicago, 2010. https://tinyurl.com/2nwssbp9.

Loritts, Bryan C. *The Offensive Church: Breaking the Cycle of Ethnic Disunity*. Downers Grove, IL: InterVarsity Press, 2023.

McKnight, Scot, and Laura Barringer. *A Church Called Tov: Forming a Goodness Culture That Resists Abuses of Power and Promotes Healing*. Carol Stream, IL: Tyndale House, 2020.

McNeil, Brenda Salter. *Roadmap to Reconciliation: Moving Communities into Unity, Wholeness and Justice*. Downers Grove, IL: InterVarsity Press, 2015.

Mills, C. Wright. *The Sociological Imagination*. New York: Oxford University Press, 1959.

Mingo, Chuck, and Troy Jackson. *Living Undivided: Loving Courageously for Racial Healing and Justice*. Grand Rapids: Baker, 2024.

Nam, Jane. "Average ACT Score." Best Colleges, January 17, 2024. https://tinyurl.com/2tub7fa6.

Perkins, John, with Karen Waddles. *One Blood: Parting Words to the Church on Race and Love*. Chicago: Moody, 2020.

Purifoye, Gwendolyn. *Race in Motion: Public Transportation and Restricted Mobile Spaces*. New York: NYU Press, 2025.

Ray, Victor. "A Theory of Racialized Organizations." *American Sociological Review* 84, no. 1 (2019): 26–53.

Reardon, Sean F., Demetra Kalogrides, and Kenneth Shores. "The Geography of Racial/Ethnic Test Score Gaps." *American Journal of Sociology* 124, no. 4 (2019): 1164–221.

Romero, Robert Chao. *Brown Church: Five Centuries of Latina/o Social Justice, Theology, and Identity*. Downers Grove, IL: InterVarsity Press, 2020.

Rowe, Sheila Wise. *Healing Racial Trauma: The Road to Resilience*. Downers Grove, IL: InterVarsity Press, 2020.

Royster, Deirdre A. *Race and the Invisible Hand: How White Networks Exclude Black Men from Blue-Collar Jobs*. Berkeley: University of California Press, 2003.

Sanchez, Michelle T. *Color-Courageous Discipleship, Student Edition*. Colorado Springs: Waterbrook, 2020.

Sanders, Alvin. *Uncommon Church: Community Transformation for the Common Good*. Downers Grove, IL: InterVarsity Press, 2020.

Shelton, Jason, and Michael O. Emerson. *Blacks and Whites in Christian*

Bibliography

America: How Racial Discrimination Shapes Religious Convictions. New York: NYU Press, 2012.

Sloman, Steven, and Philip Fernbach. *The Knowledge Illusion: Why We Never Think Alone.* New York: Riverhead, 2018.

Sunwoog, Kim. "Long-Term Appreciation of Owner-Occupied Single-Family House Prices in Milwaukee Neighborhoods." *Urban Geography* 24, no. 3 (2003): 212–31.

Swanson, David W. *Rediscipling the White Church: From Cheap Diversity to True Solidarity.* Downers Grove, IL: InterVarsity Press, 2020.

Tisby, Jemar. *How to Fight Racism: Courageous Christianity and the Journey toward Racial Justice.* Grand Rapids: Zondervan, 2021.

Twiss, Richard. *Rescuing the Gospel from the Cowboys: A Native American Expression of the Jesus Way.* Downers Grove, IL: InterVarsity Press, 2015.

Wikipedia. Altgeld Garden Homes, accessed April 2023. https://tinyurl.com/3c9x58rx.

Woodley, Randy. *Shalom and the Community of Creation: An Indigenous Vision.* Grand Rapids: Eerdmans, 2012.

Index

A&P store, 32
Action Meeting(s), 78–80, 142
Acts 2 experience, 90
Africa, 34
Air Force, 74
Altgeld Gardens neighborhood (Chicago), 16, 79, 81
  housing project, 15, 17, 21–23, 33–34, 86
American Dream, 17, 86, 98–101, 140
Anderson, Scott, 39, 40
anger, 9, 53, 66, 90, 121, 136
apartheid, 17
appraisal(s), 93, 98–99, 100–101, 111
Asian, Asians, 110, 132, 155, 163, 164
  neighborhood, 108
  students, 68, 114
Asian American Christian Collaborative, 104
atrocities, 17
attorney, 59–60
Austin neighborhood (Chicago), 76–77

bank(s), 62, 83, 86–88
  account, size of, 19
  teller, working as, 62
baseball, 1, 9, 11, 30–31, 37, 49–50, 51, 54, 130, 164
basketball, 17, 33–34, 37, 38, 40, 54–56
Bethel Gospel Tabernacle, 84
Bethel House of Prayer, 28–29, 30, 34, 84
Beverly neighborhood (Chicago), 29
Bible study/studies, 28, 30, 33, 39, 40, 130
biblical, 2, 3, 89, 103, 104, 110, 138
Black advantage(s), 42, 45, 47, 48, 129, 131, 155, 169
Black neighborhood(s), 27, 29, 100, 108
Black Stones Rangers, 26
Block, Peter, 128
block clubs, 80
board meeting(s), 28, 81
Bonhoeffer, Dietrich, 137, 151, 160
bootstraps, 23, 99
born again, 104
Bowen High School, 30

Index

Bracey, Glenn, 46
building blocks for kingdom racial change
  Building Block 1, 7, 23, 107, 169
  Building Block 2, 25, 42, 149, 169
  Building Block 3, 25, 45, 129, 155, 169
  Building Block 4, 25, 47, 129, 169
  Building Block 5, 49, 66, 155, 169
  Building Block 6, 49, 67, 107, 169
  Building Block 7, 49, 72, 129, 169
  Building Block 8, 73, 95, 129, 142, 169
  Building Block 9, 73, 98, 154, 169
  Building Block 10, 73, 101, 107, 169
  Building Block 11, 73, 101, 129, 169

California, 7, 10, 61–62
Carter, Jimmy, 55
Catholic, 13, 36, 37, 39, 43, 63, 92
Census Bureau, 157
Centers for Disease Control and Prevention (CDC), 156
Chang, Ray, 104
change agents, 103, 104
Chicago, Illinois, 1, 18, 61, 64, 74, 77, 79–80, 85, 133, 142
  Black, 22, 25, 38, 44–45, 93
  Chicagoland, 1, 34, 84, 129, 130
  Cubs, 1, 9–10, 130
  Hispanic, 45, 93
  Housing Authority, 22
  Loyola University of, 63–64
  move to, 8–12, 14, 25, 27, 130
  neighborhoods, 1–2, 12, 15, 22–23, 26–27, 29–31, 33–34, 49, 76, 81–84, 158

  State University, 50, 54–57
  transportation, 45
  University of, 64
  University of Illinois, 55
  WGN, 9
  white, 30, 45
  White Sox, 1, 130
Chicagoland, 1, 129
  Men's Unity Group, 56, 84, 154, 158
  Youth Fellowship, 34
Christ Community Church, 82
Christendom, 136, 149
Christian Fellowship, 55–56
Christ-like, 2, 122, 126
Circle Urban Ministry, 74–79
Civil Rights Movement, 140
Colorado Buffalos, 89
color-coded, 109
command(s), 90, 94, 118, 149–53, 158, 161, 167
community college, 63
community organization, 80–81, 101, 129, 149, 169
community organizer, organizing, 78, 80, 101
connection(s), 11, 49, 67–68, 71–72, 92, 95, 127, 129, 169
contact theory, 95–97
Control Data, 36
Corinthians, First Letter to the, 150
COVID-19, 93, 132
Crawford, Paul, 84
creation, 1, 3, 95, 109, 154
crime, 18, 20–21, 26, 32, 35, 57, 78–79, 97, 109, 123, 155, 158
criminal-justice system, 2, 125n15, 165

Index

cross-racial, 73, 96–98, 136, 154–55, 158, 169
Crosstown Classic, 1, 130–33
Crowder, Kyle, 20
Cummings, Terry, 33

dangerous, 18, 26, 27
Darity, William, 122
data, 2, 64, 68–69, 97, 99–100
Davis, James, 58
day cares, 80
deacon(s), 35, 81
deindustrialization, 50
DePaul University, 54–55
Detroit, Michigan, 10–11, 12–14, 18, 25, 27, 35
Developing Communities Project (DCP), 78, 80–81, 83, 142
devil, 155, 159, 161, 167
dialysis, 60, 84–85
Disneyland, 61–62
doctor, 2, 13, 35, 61, 66, 86, 116
doctorate, 65, 98, 161
downtown, 13, 18, 51, 85, 93
drugs, 16, 40, 78, 79

economy, 42, 44, 50, 110, 117
educational system, 2, 114, 126, 142
Edwards, Korie Little, 135
elders, church, 28, 161
employment, 22, 37, 53, 54, 71, 91, 128, 158
empower, 47, 94, 95, 134, 153
Englewood neighborhood, 25–27, 54
English (language), 38, 43, 116, 117, 150
Eruka organization, 110–13
ethnic enclave, 14

Evangelical Christian Church, 27, 28, 29
evangelism, 33
Evanston, Illinois, 12
exclusive, 165
executive director, 75–76, 80, 81

factory, 49
Fair Housing Act, 20
farmhouse, 91
Fernbach, Philip, 154
flourish, flourishing, 3, 34, 47, 94, 103
Ford Motor Company, 11, 12, 26
friendship(s), 28, 46–47, 96, 130, 132, 133, 136, 145, 158, 164–65
fundraising, 76–77

gang(s), 16, 22, 26–27, 32, 34, 36, 76, 155
Gangster Disciples, 26
Gary, Indiana, 85
Genesis, book of, 82
ghetto, 31, 34
GI Bill, 42, 43, 67
godly, ungodly, 2, 20, 23, 58, 103, 107, 130
God's will, 46, 83, 144–45
gospel, 20, 34, 39, 97, 136, 153
Goza, Joel, 120–24
grade school, 2, 34, 36, 55, 92, 113, 133, 158
Grier, Rosie, 75
grocery store(s), 31, 32, 44, 45, 50
Guaranteed Rate Field, 1

Harvard Law Review, 80
Harvard Law School, 79, 80
Harvard University, 80
healing, 85, 89, 110, 120

Index

heaven, 4, 46, 137, 152, 153, 167
Heinitz, Lyle, 40
Heinitz, Sandy, 40
hell, 46, 118
Hispanic, 30, 97–98, 114, 155
  Chicago, 45
  church, 133
  neighborhood(s), 93, 100, 108
  students, 68
Holloway, Scottye, 92
homelessness, 60, 63, 66, 108
Homewood-Flossmoor High School, 88
Houston, Texas, 93, 100
  Educational Research Consortium, 115
Howell, Junia, 109–13
Hyde Park neighborhood (Chicago), 79
hypertension, 61

Illinois, 10, 49, 73, 85
imprisonment, 158
inclusive, 104, 117, 164
Ingleside Community Church of the Nazarene, 83–84
inspector, 49
intrusive, 104, 165
IQ tests, 70
Isaiah, book of, 125
Italian(s), 13, 36, 37, 43, 61, 63

James, apostle, 108
James, Letter of, 107
Jesus, 118, 120, 126, 148, 149, 158
Johnson, Benjamin, 81–82
Joliet, Illinois, 85

kidney disease, 61, 84
kindergarten, 11–12, 27, 92, 115, 117

Kinder Institute, 115, 117
King, Martin Luther, Jr., 14, 140
kingdom of God, kingdom of heaven, 4, 152
kingdom racial change, definition, 2, 103. *See also* building blocks for kingdom racial change
Korver-Glenn, Elizabeth, 101, 109
Krysan, Maria, 20

lacrosse, 88
Lake Michigan, 25, 85
Lampa, Rachel, 148
leadership, 14, 77, 94–95, 164
  church, 30
  community, 78
  goal, 94
  group, 164
  poor, 94
  positions, 135
  school, 92
  skills, 55
  structures, 94, 134
  table, 164
  team, 75–76, 163–64
  training retreats, 81
Lemont High School, 88
lending, 87, 111
Lewis, Claude, 28, 29, 34, 82
"like themselves," 19, 109
loan(s), 20, 87–88, 93, 97, 101, 112, 113, 117
  application, 87
  construction, 86, 87
  debt, 117
  end, 87
  house, 87
  industry, 99
  mortgage, 87, 93
  officer, 87

Index

process, 101
system, 112
Luke, Gospel of, 126, 148, 152
lynch, lynching, 17, 88

Mark, Gospel of, 136, 152
market, 93, 99–100, 109
marriage, 16, 21, 22, 43, 44, 63
Mason-Dixon Line, 10
Mass, attending, 36
math, 55, 56, 113, 115
Matthew, Gospel of, 152
Maxwell, Clint, 53
McCartney, Bill, 89
MCAT (medical-school standardized exam), 56–57
mechanic, 7, 49, 70
Meyer, Ray, 54
Michigan, 10–11, 13, 25
military, 13, 14, 42, 43, 61
Mills, C. Wright, 41
Milwaukee, Wisconsin, 99
Minneapolis, Minnesota, 36–37, 91, 93
    Minneapolis Community College, 63
Minnesota, 36, 40, 61, 63, 65, 159
minister, 7, 33, 153
minority, 21, 90, 91, 98, 103, 121
mission, 20, 94, 110, 133–34, 136, 137
Mississippi, 91
Moody Bible Institute, 82
Morris, Illinois, 85–86
Mullen, A. Kristen, 122
multiracial, 1, 35, 132–34, 164

NAACP (National Association for the Advancement of Colored People), 59

National Institutes of Health, 157
Native American(s), 68, 97, 114, 155
    neighborhoods, 108
nephrologist(s), 60, 84, 86
nephrology, 60–61, 84–85
New Beginnings Ministry of Faith Church, 82
Norwegian, 13, 36, 37, 43

Obama, Barack, 79–81, 142
obey, obeying, 150, 151, 153

parables, 1, 4, 152
penalty, 21
person-on-the-street explanation, 19, 108
Phuket, Thailand, 163
physician(s), 56, 84–88
police, 13, 17, 26, 29, 30, 51–52, 53, 86
poverty, 15, 21–22, 100, 109, 155, 157, 158
prejudice(s), 20–21, 24, 38–39, 43, 47, 86, 95, 109, 126
prekindergarten, 115
principle, 28, 88, 92
prison, prisoners, 1, 16, 97, 126
projects, 16, 23, 32–34, 35, 55
Promise Keepers, 89
Protestant, 39, 43
Pullman neighborhood (Chicago), 81
Purifoye, Gwendolyn, 45

racial inequality, 2, 21, 69, 72, 96–97, 101–3, 111, 121, 126, 139, 167
racial injustice, 23, 107, 110, 122, 126, 133
racial minority, 21, 90, 91

Index

racial reconciliation, 74, 89, 104, 132, 133, 135
Ray, Victor, 134
Reagan, Ronald, 123–24
realtor, 20, 91
recalculation, 136–37
reenvisioning, 137
Religion of Whiteness (ROW), 25, 46, 47, 129, 135, 142, 164, 169
renew, renewing, 144–49, 158, 160, 165
repentance, 120–21, 126
restaurant(s), 10, 13, 39, 63, 76, 79, 82
Revelation, book of, 82, 161, 167
Rice University, 115, 117
riot(s), 13, 14
roadblocks, 159, 161
roller rink, 36, 37, 43
Romans, Letter to the, 144
Roseland Bible Church, 83
Roseland neighborhood (Chicago), 17, 29, 33, 79, 80, 81, 83
Royster, Deidre, 69–72

safe, safety, 14, 26, 30, 58, 156–57, 159
Salem Baptist Church, 80
Sanborn, Curt, 40
San Francisco, California, 7, 9, 11
Satan, 3, 108, 167
scholar, 64, 113, 122, 123, 140
scholarship(s), 33, 63, 68
Scripture, 34, 107n1, 126
seminary, 7, 9, 135
short sale, 93
skin, 18, 23, 29, 79, 89, 121
Sloman, Steven, 154

social justice, 63
social location(s), 25, 44, 141, 149, 153, 158, 169
  definition, 42
social media, 118, 141, 150
social structures, 95, 128
  definition, 95
sociological imagination, 41, 44
sociologist, 2, 20, 41, 134, 135
sociology, 64
South, southern, 10, 49
South Africa, 120
Southern Illinois University, 49, 50
Southern Mississippi University, 91
Springfield, Illinois, 73
standardized test(s), 38, 55, 56, 59, 67–68, 114, 116
  ACT, 63, 68
  gaps, 68
  GRE, 64
  MCAT, 56
  SAT, 68
  scores, 55, 64, 68
stereotype(s), 85, 86, 97, 131
St. Louis, Missouri, 15
St. Mark Full Gospel Church, 30
St. Paul, Minnesota, 91
street(s), 1, 27, 29, 40, 51, 53, 61–62, 108–9, 127
suburb(s), 14, 34–36, 43, 50, 61, 76, 84, 89, 91
Sunday school, 28, 30, 35, 39

teen coordinator, 74–75, 76
Thailand, 163
3D, 165–66
time frame, 141

Index

toxic, toxicity, 22–23, 160
transformed, 104, 144
Twin Cities, Minnesota, 37, 91–92

UCLA, 62
uneducated, lack of education, 43
unemployed, unemployment, 22, 81, 158
Unity in the Church (UnityInTheChurch.org), 129, 130, 133
University of Alabama at Birmingham, 60, 84
University of North Carolina, 64
University of Southern Mississippi, 91
UPS, 50–51, 53
Urban Training Institute, 81

veteran(s), 14, 22, 43
violence, 1, 13–14, 57, 140, 156
 nonviolence, 140
voter registration, 80

Washington High School, 30
wealth gap, 21, 122
West Pullman neighborhood (Chicago), 81
white flight, 27, 35, 67, 93
white neighborhood(s), 27, 29, 32, 88, 91, 100–101, 108–9
Willow Creek Church, 130–32

youth director, 74–77, 95
youth ministry, 35, 74, 94
youth program, 29, 33, 75–77